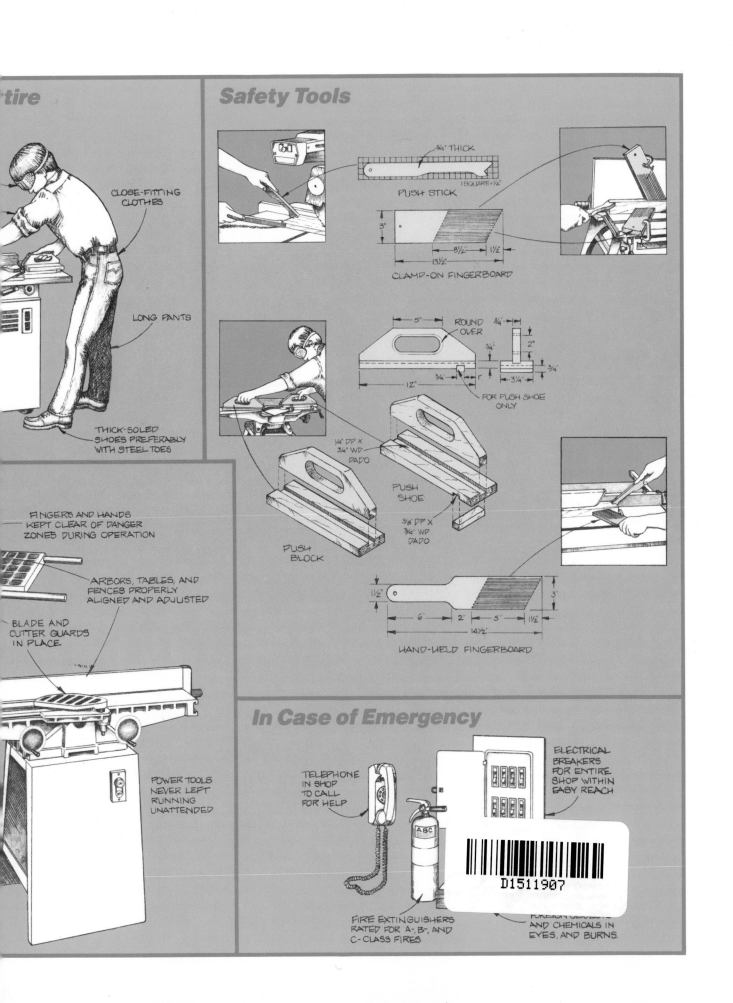

...tire

CLOSE-FITTING CLOTHES

LONG PANTS

THICK-SOLED SHOES PREFERABLY WITH STEEL TOES

FINGERS AND HANDS KEPT CLEAR OF DANGER ZONES DURING OPERATION

ARBORS, TABLES, AND FENCES PROPERLY ALIGNED AND ADJUSTED

BLADE AND CUTTER GUARDS IN PLACE

POWER TOOLS NEVER LEFT RUNNING UNATTENDED

Safety Tools

¾" THICK

1 SQUARE = ½"

PUSH STICK

3"

8½" 1½"

13½"

CLAMP-ON FINGERBOARD

5" ROUND OVER ¾"

¾" 2"

12" ¾" r 3¼" ¾"

FOR PUSH SHOE ONLY

¼" DP X ¾" WD DADO

PUSH SHOE

⅜" DP X ¾" WD DADO

PUSH BLOCK

1½" 3"

6" 2" 5" 1½"

14½"

HAND-HELD FINGERBOARD

In Case of Emergency

ELECTRICAL BREAKERS FOR ENTIRE SHOP WITHIN EASY REACH

TELEPHONE IN SHOP TO CALL FOR HELP

ABC

FIRE EXTINGUISHERS RATED FOR A-, B-, AND C-CLASS FIRES

FOREIGN OBJECTS AND CHEMICALS IN EYES, AND BURNS.

·BUILD·IT·BETTER·YOURSELF·
WOODWORKING PROJECTS

Tables and Chairs

Collected and Written
by Nick Engler

Rodale Press
Emmaus, Pennsylvania

If you have any questions or comments concerning this book, please write:
Rodale Press
Book Reader Service
33 East Minor Street
Emmaus, PA 18098

Series Editor: Jeff Day
Managing Editor/Author: Nick Engler
Editor: Roger Yepsen
Copy Editors: Mary Green
Sally L. Schaffer
Graphic Designer: Linda Watts
Graphic Artists: Mary Jane Favorite
Chris Walendzak
Photography: Karen Callahan
Cover Photography: Mitch Mandel
Cover Photograph Stylist: Janet C. Vera
Proofreader: Hue Park
Typesetting by Computer Typography, Huber Heights, Ohio
Interior Illustrations by Scot T. Marsh and O'Neil & Associates, Dayton, Ohio
Endpaper Illustrations by Mary Jane Favorite
Produced by Bookworks, Inc., West Milton, Ohio

Library of Congress Cataloging-in-Publication Data

Engler, Nick.
Tables and chairs / collected and written by Nick Engler.
p. cm. — (Build-it-better-yourself woodworking projects)
ISBN 0–87857–945–1 hardcover
1. Tables. 2. Chairs. I. Title. II. Series: Engler, Nick. Build-it-better-yourself woodworking projects.
TT197.5.T3E54 1991
684.1′3—dc20
90–25287
CIP

6 8 10 9 7   hardcover

Contents

Table and Chair Ergonomics

Perhaps the most important task when building a table or chair is to make the project a pleasure to use. No one will spend much time sitting in an uncomfortable chair or working at an awkward table. The furniture must fit the user properly, making him or her feel relaxed.

Building comfortable furniture is not difficult, as long as you follow a few simple guidelines. It was once a matter of trial and error for old-time furnituremakers, but no longer. During the last half of this century, we've made comfort into a science and given it a name — *ergonomics.* Good ergonomics is a simple matter of proportion — knowing the proper size and orientation of each piece of a project, and how it affects the other pieces.

Chair Proportions

When building a chair, the first consideration is the seat. The most important proportions of a seat are the *height, depth,* and *width,* in that order. It's generally accepted that the average adult man feels most comfortable when sitting in a seat that is 18″ high. The average woman prefers one that is 15″ high. Most furnituremakers compromise and build chairs 16″ tall. If you want to design a seat for a specific person, place the seat so the user's feet will be flat on the ground when he or she sits up straight.

The depth of the seat should be 16¾″ to 18½″. If it's too deep, the front edge will press on the back of the knees. If it's too shallow, the seat won't properly support the sitter's weight. The width should allow at least 16½″ to 20″ for each person who will sit on the seat. For example, a bench or settee that is intended to accommodate two people should be at least 37″ wide.

The angles of the seat and back are also very important. If the seat has no back, it should be horizontal — parallel to the ground. If it has a back, the seat should tilt toward the back 5° to 8°. This slope helps to support the pelvis and the lumbar curve of the spine in a natural position. If the back is low — 8″ or less — the back posts should be perpendicular to the ground. Taller backs should slant at an angle of 70° to 80° (as mea-

sured from the ground). This helps to support the shoulders. Easy chairs — chairs meant for relaxing — may have seats and backs that slope at steeper angles.

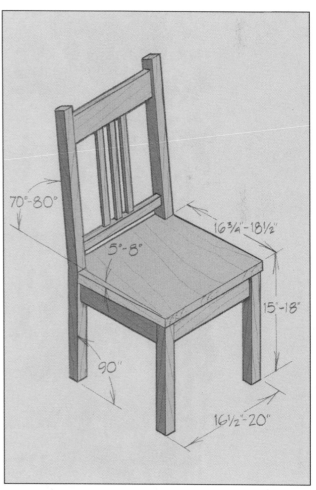

When designing and building a seat, pay close attention to the proportions — height, depth, and width. If the seat has a back, consider the angle of the surfaces that support your weight when seated.

Table Proportions

The most important dimension of a table is the height of the top. This will vary depending on how the table is used. Generally, tabletops should be 27″ to 29″ above the floor. This is a good height for dining, writing, working, and most tasks that you perform while sitting. The exception to this rule is typing — the surface must be lower so your hands will rest comfortably on top of the keyboard. Tables that hold typewriters and computers should be 25″ to 27″ high.

Workbenches and kitchen counters — tables at which you stand to work — should be 33″ to 36″ high. Coffee tables, side tables, and end tables are 12″ to 22″ high. You want these tabletops and whatever they support to be well below your line of sight when you're sitting down, so you'll be able to carry on a conversation over them. Small, occasional tables can be almost any height, depending on what they hold.

When making dining tables or other tables at which more than one person will sit, you must allow enough room for each person to be comfortable. Generally, each person should have 23″ side to side (along the edge of the table), and at least 12″ from the edge to the center of the table. Certain shapes require special considerations. For example, to accommodate four people, square tables should be at least 30″ to a side, and round tables should be at least 36″ in diameter.

There are some important dimensions under the table, also. The bottom edge of the apron should be at least 21″ to 24″ above the floor to allow clearance for knees. Each person should have 18″ to 24″ from the edge of the table to make room for his or her toes. Unlike the space on the top of the table, one person's toe space can overlap another's — people sitting opposite one another will instinctively arrange their feet so as not to step on one another's toes.

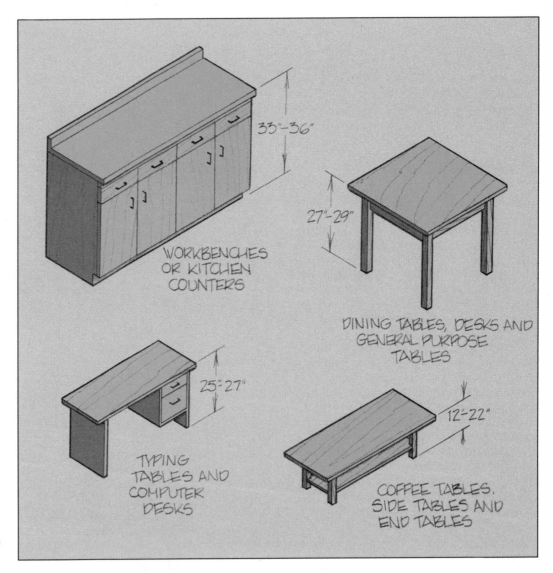

The height of a tabletop will depend on how you use the table.

Departures

You won't be able to design or build every chair or table to these precise proportions, of course. You may be limited by materials, available space, and other factors. Or you may wish to experiment with nontradition-al forms and styles. Many of the designs in this book depart from the norms for one reason or another. But you should understand these basics and use them as a reference or jumping-off point. This will help you focus on the true purpose of every chair and table — to make the world a more comfortable place.

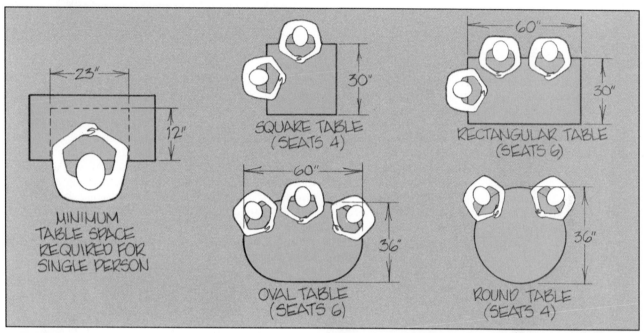

When designing a table at which more than one person will sit, you must provide adequate space for each.

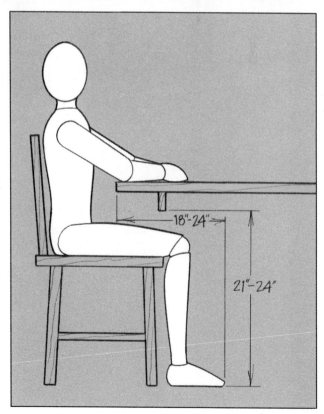

In addition to space on top of the table, each person also needs his or her own space under it.

Harvest Table

Surprisingly, there are very few examples of large dining tables from seventeenth- and eighteenth-century America. Since most colonial homes were extremely small by contemporary standards, space was at a premium. Consequently, dining tables were also small. Large families ate in shifts, except for a few special occasions when they all celebrated together. During those occasions, they made large "harvest" tables by laying two or three wide boards across sawbucks.

During the early nineteenth century, when life in America was more settled and prosperous, houses and tables became larger. Many of these larger tables were reminiscent of the old makeshift plank tables — three wide boards arranged edge to edge. Some could be broken down to save space between meals, like the old tables. (After all, the houses weren't *that* much larger.) Usually, the two outside boards were hinged so that they folded down when the table wasn't in use. Because of these similarities, the new tables also were called harvest tables — the name we know them by today.

The harvest table shown was built in the early nineteenth century by an Ohio cabinetmaker. It will seat two people with both leaves folded down, five people with one leaf up, and eight people with both leaves up.

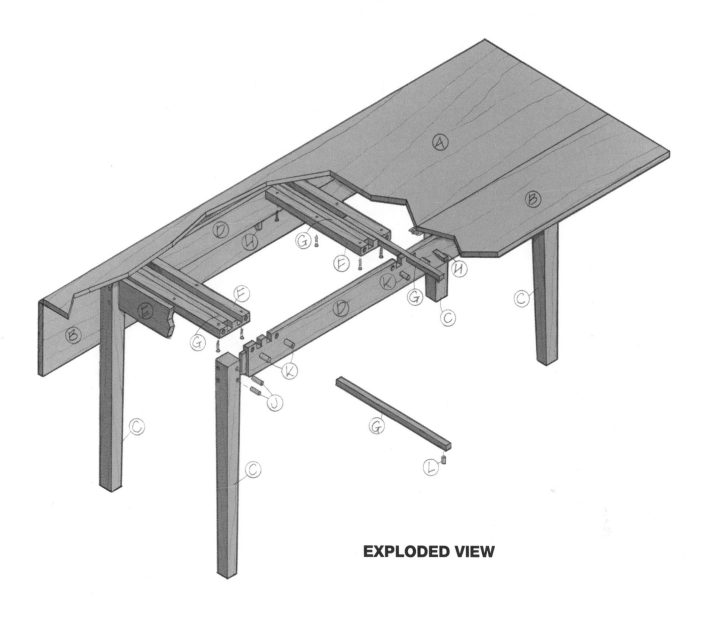

EXPLODED VIEW

Materials List

FINISHED DIMENSIONS

PARTS

A.	Top	3/4" x 20" x 72"
B.	Leaves (2)	3/4" x 10" x 72"
C.	Legs (4)	2 1/8" x 2 1/8" x 29"
D.	Long aprons (2)	3/4" x 4" x 52"
E.	Short aprons (2)	3/4" x 4" x 16 3/4"
F.	Slide housings (3)	1 x 4 3/4" x 16"
G.	Slides (6)	11/16" x 11/16" x 19"
H.	Wedges (6)	3/4" x 3/4" x 2 3/8"
J.	Leg dowels (16)	3/8" dia. x 1 1/2"
K.	Slide housing dowels (12)	1/2" dia. x 1 1/2"
L.	Slide dowels (6)	3/8" dia. x 3/4"

HARDWARE

#10 x 1 1/2" Flathead wood screws (18)

#8 x 1 1/4" Flathead wood screws (6)

2 1/2" x 1 1/4" Brass hinges and mounting screws (8)

1

***Select the stock and cut the parts to
size.*** To make this table, you need approximately 27 board feet of 4/4 (four-quarters) stock, 3
board feet of 5/4 (five-quarters) stock, and 7 board feet
of 10/4 (ten-quarters) stock, plus one $3/8$″-diameter, 36″-
long dowel and one $1/2$″-diameter, 36″-long dowel. You
can make this project from almost any cabinet-grade
hardwood, but most historical examples were made
from cherry or maple. (The top, legs, and aprons on the
table shown are made of maple.) Choose an *extremely*
hard, strong wood for the slides, preferably a species
with a little give. The slides on this table are made from
hickory.

Plane the 4/4 stock to $3/4$″ thick and glue up the
boards needed to make the top. Cut the top, leaves,
aprons, and wedges to size. Plane a large scrap of $1/2$″-
thick stock to $11/16$″ and cut the slides to size. Plane the
5/4 stock to 1″ and cut the slide housings to size. Also,
cut the dowels to length.

Rip the $2\frac{1}{2}$″-wide, $2\frac{1}{2}$″-thick leg blanks from the 10/4
stock. Joint two adjacent surfaces of each blank so
they're perfectly straight and precisely 90° from one
another. Mark the jointed sides with a pencil. Plane the
remaining two sides, removing stock until the blanks
are $2\frac{1}{8}$″ square. Be careful *not* to remove the pencil
marks as you plane. Cut the legs to the proper length.

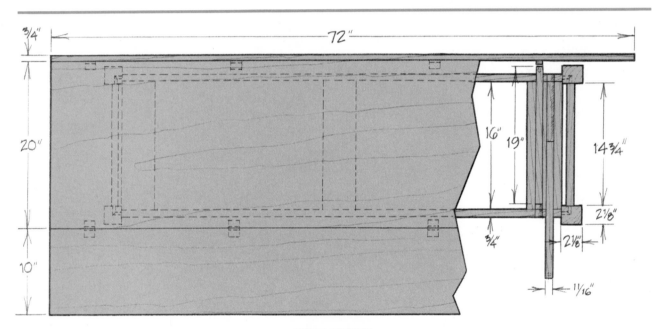

TOP VIEW

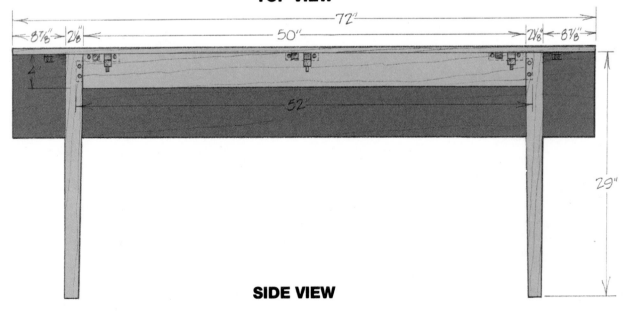

SIDE VIEW

TRY THIS! To minimize cupping, make sure the annual rings on the top and leaves curve *up* as you look at the end grain. You might also make the top and leaves from quarter-sawn (or rift-sawn) lumber. This is more expensive than plain-sawn stock, but it's very stable and won't cup.

2 Cut the mortises and tenons in the legs and aprons.

The legs are joined to the aprons by mortise-and-tenon joints. Cut the mortises in the legs first, then fit the apron tenons to them.

Lay out the ¼″-wide, 3″-long, 1″-deep mortises on the leg stock near the upper ends, as shown in the *Leg Layout*. Remove most of the stock from each mortise by drilling a series of overlapping holes. Clean up the sides and square the ends of the mortises with a chisel.

You can also rout the mortises with a table-mounted or side-mounted router. Mark *all four* surfaces of each leg so you know where to start and stop cutting each mortise. Stick a piece of masking tape on the router table and, using a square, mark the diameter of the router bit on the tape. (See Figure 1.) Clamp a fence to the table to guide the cut and adjust the height of the bit so it's just ⅛″ above the table surface. Turn the router on and, holding the leg firmly against the fence, slowly

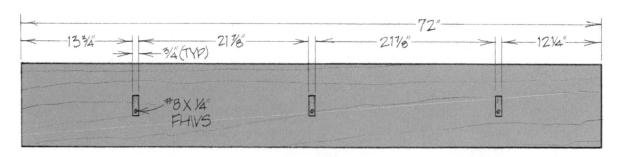

BOTTOM VIEW
LEAF LAYOUT

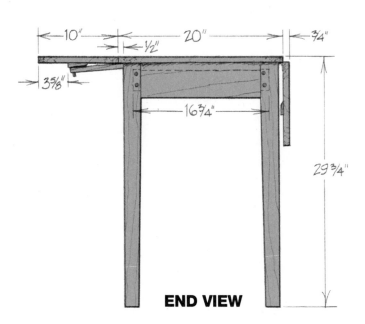

END VIEW

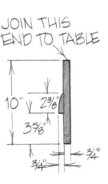

END VIEW

and carefully lower it onto the bit. The bit should be approximately centered in the mortise. (See Figure 2.) Feed the leg left and right, cutting the entire length of the mortise. (See Figure 3.) Then repeat for the remaining mortises. Turn the router off, raise the bit another $\frac{1}{8}''$, and repeat. Continue until you have routed all eight mortises 1″ deep. Square the ends of each mortise with a chisel.

Cut the $\frac{1}{4}''$-thick, 3″-wide, 1″-long tenons in the ends of the aprons, using a dado cutter or a table-mounted router. Mark the length of each tenon on all four surfaces of the apron with a marking gauge — this will prevent the wood from chipping or tearing out as you remove the stock. To form a tenon on the end of the board, cut a 1″-wide, $\frac{1}{4}''$-deep rabbet in one face of the apron, turn it over, and cut a matching rabbet in the opposite face.

Make a practice tenon in a scrap of $1\frac{3}{4}''$-thick stock first. Fit this tenon to one of the mortises. If it's too tight, raise the bit or cutter slightly. If it's too loose, lower the bit or cutter. Cut another practice tenon and fit it to the mortise again. Repeat until the tenon fits properly, then cut all the tenons in the ends of the aprons.

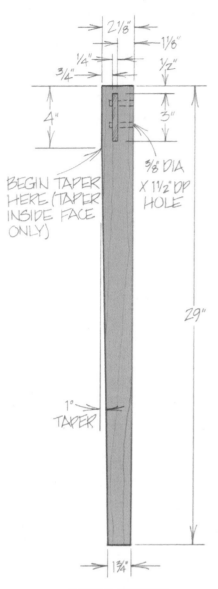

LEG LAYOUT

1/So you know when to stop cutting, mark the top and bottom of the mortise on all four surfaces of the leg stock. Also, mark the diameter of the bit on the router table.

2/Hold the leg firmly against the fence and lower it onto the bit. Lower it very slowly so the bit doesn't catch the leg and kick it to the right or left.

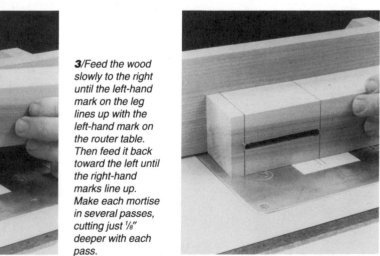

3/Feed the wood slowly to the right until the left-hand mark on the leg lines up with the left-hand mark on the router table. Then feed it back toward the left until the right-hand marks line up. Make each mortise in several passes, cutting just $\frac{1}{8}''$ deeper with each pass.

3 Cut the notches in the long aprons.

The top edges of the long aprons are notched to accommodate the slides. Since both aprons are notched identically, you can cut their notches at the same time.

Stick the two boards together, inside face to inside face, with double-faced carpet tape. Make sure the ends and the edges are flush. Lay out the notches, as shown in the *Long Apron Layout,* on the top board in the stack.

Cut the notches with a dado cutter or table-mounted router, using a miter gauge to guide the wood. Attach an extra long extension to the miter gauge, then clamp the aprons to the extension. Feed the wood slowly into the bit or cutter. (See Figure 4.) If you're using a table-mounted router, cut each notch in several passes, raising the cutter ⅛"–¼" with each pass.

4/To help keep the aprons perpendicular to the cutter as you make the notches, attach an extension to the miter gauge, then clamp the aprons to this extension.

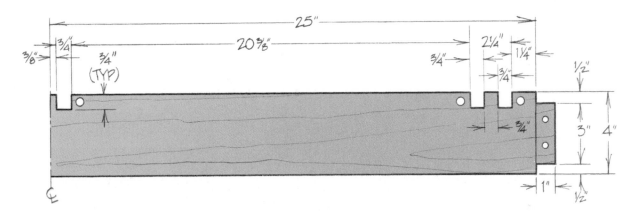

SIDE VIEW

LONG APRON LAYOUT

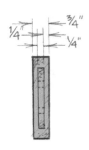

END VIEW

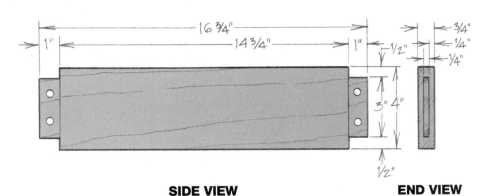

SIDE VIEW   **END VIEW**

SHORT APRON LAYOUT

4 **_Cut the grooves and drill the holes in the slide housings._** The slides rest in three slide housings. There are two slides in each housing, and they travel in and out of grooves. Cut these ³⁄₄″-wide, ³⁄₄″-deep grooves with a dado cutter or table-mounted router, as shown in the _Slide Housing Layout_. Remember, these grooves must be spaced _precisely_ the

same as the notches in the top edges of the aprons.

After cutting the grooves, drill six ¹⁄₄″-diameter holes through the housings, as shown in the layout. You'll use these holes later to attach the top to the table. The spacing of these holes is not critical, but there should be two near the middle and two near each end of each apron.

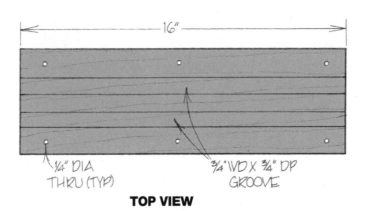

TOP VIEW   END VIEW

SLIDE HOUSING LAYOUT

5 **_Cut the tapers in the legs._** Each leg tapers from 2¹⁄₈″ square at the top to 1³⁄₄″ square at the bottom. Cut these tapers on a table saw or band saw. If you use a table saw, set up a tapering jig to hold the legs at a slight angle to the blade. (See Figure 5.) Start each taper 4″ below the top end of the leg, as shown in the _Leg Layout_. Taper the _inside_ surfaces of the legs only. For more information on cutting tapers, refer to Step-by-Step: Making Tapered Legs.

5/If you cut the tapers on a table saw, use a tapering jig to hold the wood at the proper angle to the blade. Guide the jig along the fence as you feed the wood. Begin the tapers 4″ from the top of each leg on the **inside** surfaces only.

6 **_Cut the shapes of the wedges._** The wedges on the undersides of the leaves serve two purposes. First, they prevent someone from pulling the slides all the way out of the housings once the table is assembled. They also keep the raised leaves flush with the top, since the slides tend to droop slightly when extended.

To make the wedges, enlarge the side pattern in the _Wedge Layout_. Trace the pattern onto the stock and cut the shape with a band saw or scroll saw. Sand the sawed edges.

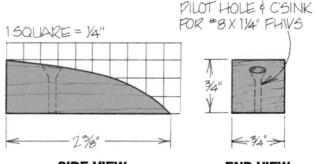

SIDE VIEW   END VIEW

WEDGE LAYOUT

7

Assemble the legs and aprons. Finish sand all the parts of the table. Be careful not to round over any adjoining edges or ends. Then glue the apron tenons into the leg mortises and clamp the parts together. As you tighten the clamps, check that the long aprons are square to the short ones. If not, readjust the position of the clamps.

Let the glue dry completely, then remove the clamps. Drilling from the outside surface of the leg, bore two ³⁄₈″-diameter, 1¹⁄₂″-deep holes through each mortise and tenon. Glue a ³⁄₈″-diameter, 1¹⁄₂″-long dowel in each hole and sand the ends of the dowels flush with the surfaces of the legs. This will peg the legs and aprons together.

8

Attach the slide housings to the long aprons. Position the slide housings so the grooves line up with the notches in the aprons. Glue and clamp the housings to the aprons. These glue joints won't be particularly strong — gluing end grain to long grain always makes for a weak joint — but they will be sufficient to hold the housings in place while you install the dowels.

When the glue dries, remove the clamps and drill two ¹⁄₂″-diameter, 1¹⁄₂″-deep holes through the apron and

into each end of each housing, as shown in the *Leg, Apron, and Slide Housing Assembly Detail*. Glue a ¹⁄₂″-diameter, 1¹⁄₂″-long dowel in each hole and sand the ends of the dowels flush with the surfaces of the aprons. These dowels will support the housings.

Check that the sides and bottoms of the slide housing grooves are flush with the sides and bottom of the notches. If not, file the surfaces until they are flush. *This is very important!* The slides may not operate properly if these surfaces are not flush.

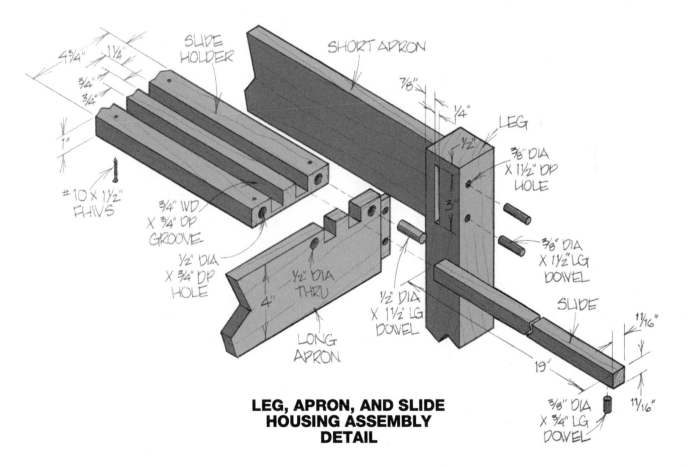

**LEG, APRON, AND SLIDE
HOUSING ASSEMBLY
DETAIL**

9 **Attach the top and leaves to the table.** Turn the tabletop upside down on the workbench. Turn the leaves upside down and place one on each side of the top. Make sure the edges butt against one another and the ends are flush, then hold them in place with bar clamps.

Mark the locations of the hinges on the undersides of the top and leaves. These locations are not critical, but there should be four hinges to each leaf, evenly spaced along the edge. The barrel of each hinge should straddle the joint between the leaf and the top. Cut a mortise for each hinge and install it so the hinge leaves are flush with the wood surface.

Turn the leg-and-apron assembly upside down and center it on the top. Drive #10 x 1½″ flathead wood screws through the holes in the slide housings and into the top. Note that these holes are slightly larger than the shanks of the screws. This will allow the top to expand and contract with changes in the weather. Tighten the screws so they're snug, but not so tight as to keep the top from moving.

10 **Install the slides and wedges.** Drill a ³⁄₈″-diameter, ³⁄₈″-deep hole in one end of each slide, as shown in the *Slide End Detail*. Glue a ³⁄₈″-diameter, ³⁄₄″-long dowel in each hole. Insert the other end of each slide into one of the notches in the long aprons. The dowel should face up, away from the top. Push the slides in until the dowels stop them.

Pull each slide out again about 7″ and mark where it rests on the leaf. Clamp the wedges to the leaves and secure them with #8 x 1¼″ flathead wood screws. Countersink the heads of the screws. Each wedge should be 3⁵⁄₈″ in from the outside edge of its leaf and centered between a set of marks. Do *not* glue the wedges in place. Should a slide crack or break, you may want to remove a wedge to replace it.

Turn the table right side up, resting on its legs. Test the action of the slides and the leaves. When the leaves are folded down, they should hang nearly perpendicu-

SLIDE END DETAIL

lar to the tabletop. When folded up, the surfaces of the leaves and top should be flush. The slides should move in and out of their housing freely. When out, they should engage the wedges slightly, holding the leaves flush to the top.

11 **Finish the table.** When you're satisfied the leaves and slides work properly, disassemble the table, removing the top, leaves, slides, and hinges. Do any necessary finish sanding, then apply a finish to all wooden surfaces, inside *and* outside, top *and* bottom. Be careful to apply as many coats to the bottoms of the top and leaves as you do the tops — this will help prevent them from cupping. Don't let the finish build up inside the grooves in the slide housings — wipe most of it away before it dries, otherwise the slides may stick.

When the finish dries, buff it out with wax. Rub a coat of paraffin wax into the slide housing grooves to help the slides move smoothly. Replace the slides in their grooves. Fasten the leaves to the top, center the top on the legs and aprons, and secure it with screws.

Dining Booth

Restaurant owners and managers have long known that the best way to pack a lot of people into a little bit of space is to put them in a *booth*. Dining booths make efficient use of space, taking up less room than a table and chairs. Yet they're every bit as comfortable.

A dining booth is the indoor cousin of the picnic table. The table space and the seating are combined in one assembly. The booth shown is a large, open-sided plywood box that encloses two benches and a table. For comfort, the benches have simple cushions — pads of foam rubber covered with upholstery cloth.

This booth was designed and built by Lewis Gay of McKee, Kentucky. As shown, the back and one side butt up against walls and are only a single layer of plywood thick. The other side is freestanding and, as such, is much thicker. However, the design is easily adapted to your house. You can butt any part of it against a wall, or make any part freestanding. You can also change the size of the booth to fit the available space.

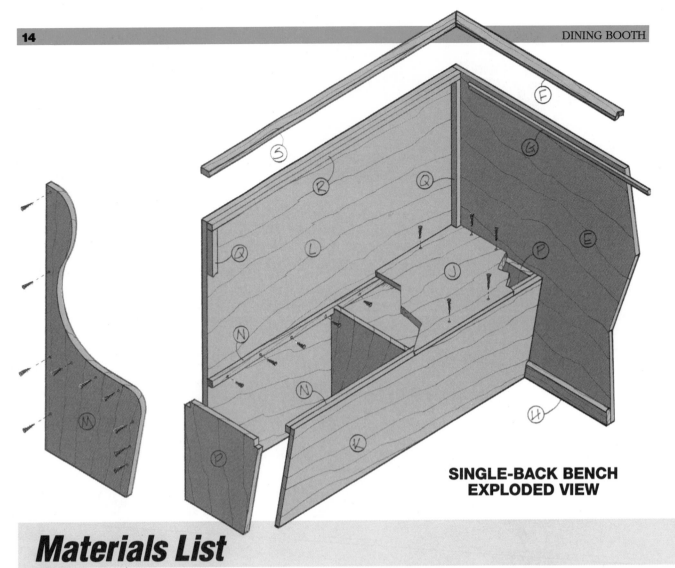

**SINGLE-BACK BENCH
EXPLODED VIEW**

Materials List

FINISHED DIMENSIONS

PARTS

Table

A. Tabletop* $1^{3}/_{4}"$ x 28" x $42^{1}/_{2}"$

B. Mounting block $^{3}/_{4}"$ x 6" x 6"

C. Leg 4" dia. x $26^{1}/_{4}"$

D. Tabletop cleat $^{3}/_{4}"$ x $1^{1}/_{2}"$ x 24"

E. Booth back* $^{3}/_{4}"$ x $41^{3}/_{4}"$ x 62"

F. Back top trim $^{3}/_{4}"$ x $1^{3}/_{4}"$ x $59^{1}/_{2}"$

G. Cove molding $^{3}/_{4}"$ x $^{3}/_{4}"$ x 58"

H. Base molding $^{3}/_{4}"$ x $3^{1}/_{4}"$ x $36^{1}/_{2}"$

Single-Back Bench

J. Seat* $^{3}/_{4}"$ x 15" x $41^{1}/_{4}"$

K. Toeboard* $^{3}/_{4}"$ x $15^{3}/_{4}"$ x $41^{1}/_{4}"$

L. Bench back* $^{3}/_{4}"$ x $41^{1}/_{4}"$ x $41^{3}/_{4}"$

M. Single-back bench end* $^{3}/_{4}"$ x $16^{5}/_{8}"$ x $41^{1}/_{4}"$

N. Seat cleats (2) $^{3}/_{4}"$ x $^{3}/_{4}"$ x $41^{1}/_{4}"$

P. Bench braces (3) $^{3}/_{4}"$ x $14^{1}/_{4}"$ x $15^{1}/_{2}"$

Q. Bench back stiles (2) $^{3}/_{4}"$ x $^{3}/_{4}"$ x $24^{3}/_{4}"$

R. Bench back rail $^{3}/_{4}"$ x $^{3}/_{4}"$ x $41^{1}/_{4}"$

S. Single-back bench top trim $^{3}/_{4}"$ x $1^{3}/_{4}"$ x $43^{1}/_{4}"$

Double-Back Bench

J. Seat* $^{3}/_{4}"$ x 15" x $41^{3}/_{4}"$

K. Toeboard* $^{3}/_{4}"$ x $15^{3}/_{4}"$ x $41^{1}/_{4}"$

L. Bench back* $^{3}/_{4}"$ x $41^{1}/_{4}"$ x $41^{3}/_{4}"$

N. Seat cleats (2) $^{3}/_{4}"$ x $^{3}/_{4}"$ x $41^{1}/_{4}"$

P. Bench braces (3) $^{3}/_{4}"$ x $14^{1}/_{4}"$ x $15^{1}/_{2}"$

Q. Bench back stiles (2) $^{3}/_{4}"$ x $^{3}/_{4}"$ x $24^{3}/_{4}"$

R. Bench back rail $^{3}/_{4}"$ x $^{3}/_{4}"$ x $41^{1}/_{4}"$

T. Double-back bench end* $^{3}/_{4}"$ x $19^{1}/_{8}"$ x $41^{1}/_{4}"$

U. Wall plates (2) $1^{1}/_{2}"$ x $1^{3}/_{4}"$ x $41^{1}/_{4}"$

V. Wall studs (4) $1^{1}/_{2}"$ x $1^{3}/_{4}"$ x $38^{3}/_{4}"$

W. Outside wall* $^{3}/_{4}"$ x $41^{3}/_{4}"$ x 42"

X. Double-back bench top trim $^{3}/_{4}"$ x $5^{1}/_{2}"$ x $43^{1}/_{4}"$

Y. Left/right wall molding $^{3}/_{4}"$ x $1^{7}/_{8}"$ x $40^{5}/_{8}"$

Z. Top wall molding $^{3}/_{4}"$ x $1^{7}/_{8}"$ x $42^{3}/_{4}"$

AA. Bottom wall molding $^{3}/_{4}"$ x $3^{1}/_{4}"$ x $40^{1}/_{2}"$

*Make these parts from plywood.

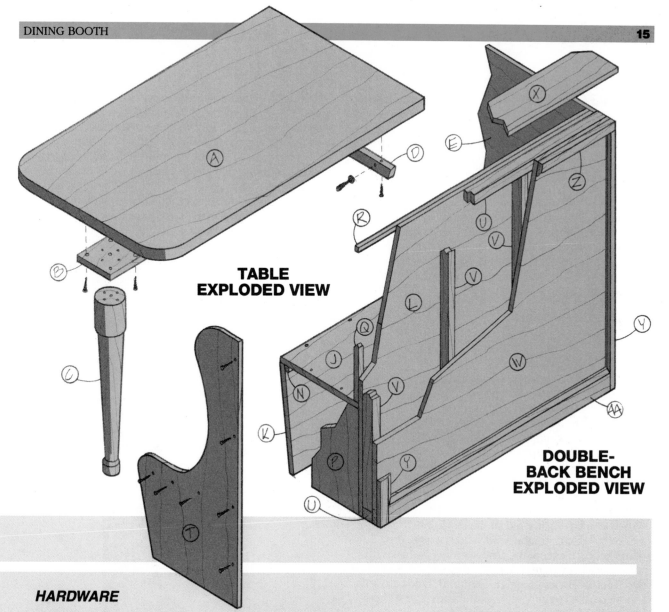

TABLE
EXPLODED VIEW

DOUBLE-
BACK BENCH
EXPLODED VIEW

HARDWARE

Table

Plastic laminate (4' x 4' sheet)
$1/4$" x 2" Lag screws (3)
$1/4$" Flat washers (3)
#12 x 3" Flathead wood screws (5)
#10 x 2" Flathead wood screws (4)
#10 x $2\frac{1}{2}$" Flathead wood screws (12–16)
#10 x $1\frac{1}{4}$" Flathead wood screws (8–12)
4d Finishing nails (18–24)

Single-Back Bench

#10 x $2\frac{1}{2}$" Flathead wood screws (8–12)
#10 x $1\frac{1}{4}$" Flathead wood screws (40–48)
4d Finishing nails (24–36)
$3/4$" Edge banding (120")
Foam rubber pads (2, to fit seat and back)
Upholstery cloth (6 yards)
Velcro™ fasteners (8–12)

Double-Back Bench

#10 x $2\frac{1}{2}$" Flathead wood screw (4–6)
#10 x $1\frac{1}{4}$" Flathead wood screws (40–48)
16d Common nails (12–16)
$1/4$" Lead shields (optional)
$1/4$" x 3" Lag screws and flat washers (optional)
4d Finishing nails (40–48)
$3/4$" Edge banding (120")
Foam rubber pads (2, to fit seat and back)
Upholstery cloth (6 yards)
Velcro™ fasteners (8–12)

1 Adapt the booth design to fit your home.

As shown, the booth is large enough for four people and requires about 20 square feet of floor space. It's nestled in a corner, so only one of the sides is free-standing. You may have to adapt this design to your home, depending on the available space and the surrounding walls.

Measure the area you've set aside for the booth and decide where you will put the booth entrance. If you need to adjust the size, then change the length of the benches or the width of the table. These components can be as long or as wide as you need; however, don't make the table any narrower than 24″ or the benches any shorter than 20″.

Decide which of the three booth sides you'll attach to an existing wall, and which must be freestanding. Any side can be attached to a wall or made freestanding. You'll need just a single sheet of plywood for those sides that you attach. But you must build a 2 x 2 frame and cover it with two sheets of plywood to make a freestanding side.

When you decide how to build your booth, make the necessary changes to the plans. Adjust the dimensions and the construction as needed. If you make extensive changes, you should draft a new set of drawings. These don't need to be professionally drafted — just something you can refer to as you build.

2 Select the stock and cut the parts to size.

To make the project as drawn, you'll need four 4′ x 8′ sheets of ³⁄₄″ cabinet-grade plywood, one 4 x 4 sheet of ¹⁄₄″ cabinet-grade plywood, two 8′-long, construction-grade 2 x 4s, about 12 board feet of 4/4 (four-quarters) cabinet-grade lumber, and a 4″ x 4″ x 30″ turning square. You can use almost any wood for the cabinet-grade stock, but the plywood and solid wood should match. The booth shown is built from birch and birch-veneer plywood.

When you have gathered all the stock, plane the 4/4 stock to ³⁄₄″ thick. Rip the solid wood parts to the widths needed, except the cove molding — make this from a wide scrap later on. Bevel the edges of the front seat cleats at 78°, as shown in *Section B*. Don't cut any of these parts to length until you're ready to use them. If the walls of your home are not perfectly square or plumb, you may have to compensate for this as you build, adjusting the long dimensions slightly.

Cut the plywood parts to the sizes needed. Bevel the top and bottom edges of the toeboards at 78°. Laminate two layers of ³⁄₄″ plywood and one layer of ¹⁄₄″ plywood to make the thick stock needed for the tabletop.

3 Attach the unsupported sides to the walls.

Attach the single-thickness bench back(s) and/or booth back to the wall studs with #10 x 2¹⁄₂″ flathead wood screws. Position the screws so they won't show when the booth is completed.

Note: Countersink all the screws in this project so the heads are flush with the wood surface, unless otherwise instructed.

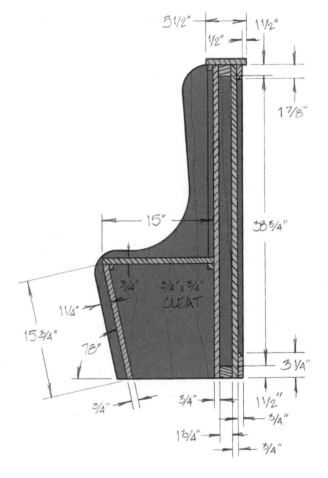

SECTION B

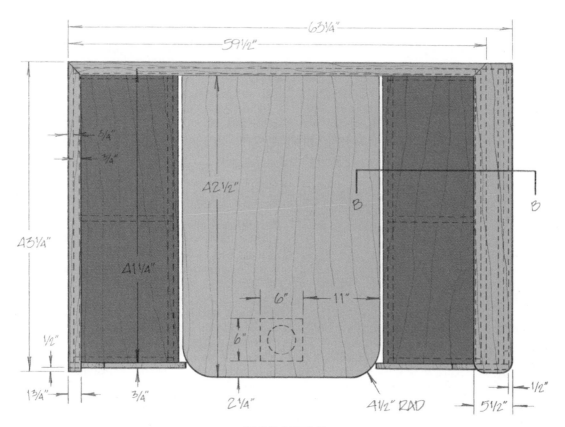

TOP VIEW

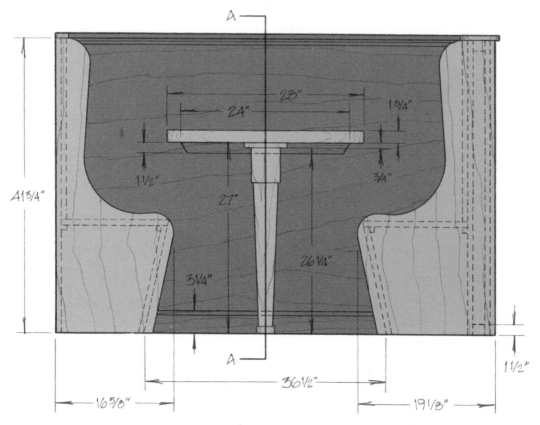

FRONT VIEW

4 **Install the freestanding sides.** Cut the 2 x 2s to the proper length, and build the free-standing side frame(s) you need, assembling the studs and plates with 16d nails. Using #10 x 2½″ flathead wood screws, secure the frames to the plywood on the unsupported walls and — if you've built more than one frame — to each other. You may also want to anchor the frames to the floor, particularly if more than one side is freestanding. If the project rests on a wood floor, secure the frames with 16d nails. If the floor is cement, use expandable lead shields and lag screws.

When the frames are installed, cover them with plywood. Attach the bench back(s) and outside wall(s) with 4d finishing nails. Set the heads of the nails.

5 **Install the benches.** Cut the cleats to the proper length. Lay out the braces on the ply-wood, as shown in the *Bench Brace Layout*. You'll need one brace at each end of each bench, and an additional brace in the middle if the benches are over 24″ in length. Cut the braces with a band saw, saber saw, or hand saw.

Fasten the back seat cleats to the plywood bench backs with glue and #10 x 1¼″ flathead wood screws. Assemble the toeboards, braces, and front seat cleats with glue and #10 x 1¼″ flathead wood screws to make two bench assemblies. Counterbore *and* countersink the *visible* screws in these assemblies (those that will show in the completed booth). The heads should be slightly below the surface of the plywood. Cover them with wooden plugs and sand the plugs flush with the surface.

Slide the assemblies in place and fasten the braces to the booth backs and the back seat cleats. Then attach the seats to the bench assemblies. Once again, counterbore and countersink the screws, and cover the heads. Also, glue veneer banding to the front edges of the seats to hide the plies. This banding should match the plywood.

6 **Turn the table leg.** Mount the leg stock square on a lathe and turn the shape shown in the *Leg Layout*. You may also turn a shape of your own design, if you wish. Finish sand the leg on the lathe.

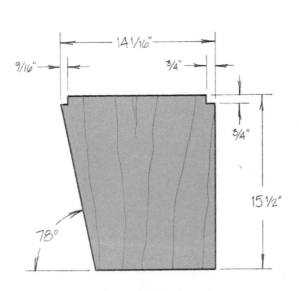

BENCH BRACE LAYOUT

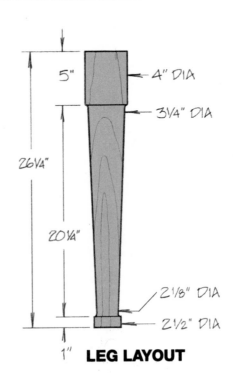

LEG LAYOUT

7 **Cover the tabletop with laminate.** On the booth shown, the plywood tabletop is covered with a plastic laminate. This not only hides the plies but it also protects and waterproofs the top. The laminate shown matches the wood in the booth, but you can use any color or design that suits you.

Cut the shape of the tabletop as shown in the *Top View,* and sand the edges. Apply laminate first to the front and side edges — you don't have to cover the back edge, because it won't be seen. Cut a long strip of laminate about 2″ wide. Spread contact cement on the table edges *and* the back of the laminate. Be careful when you spread this cement — brush it on quickly and evenly, in one pass. Do *not* go back over and brush areas where you've already applied cement, or the cement will ball up.

Let the cement dry for about 15 minutes, then apply the laminate to the edge, bending it around the curved corners. Go back and roll the laminate with a veneer roller or rolling pin. Press very hard with the roller, the harder the better. Contact cement is pressure sensitive — the more pressure you exert, the better the bond will be. When the laminate is secured to the edge, trim it to

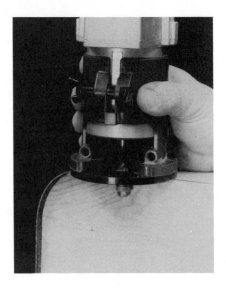

1/Trim the laminate to its final size **after** you've applied it to the tabletop. Use a hand-held router and a piloted trim bit to cut it.

its final width with a hand-held router and a piloted flush trim bit. (See Figure 1.)

Repeat this procedure for the top surface. Cut the laminate a little longer and wider than you need, then attach it with contact cement. Trim it with a flush trim or bevel trim bit.

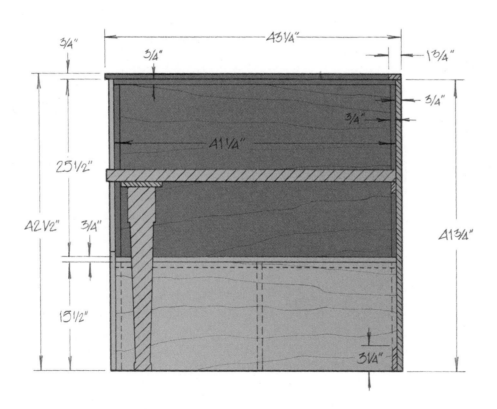

SECTION A

8   ***Assemble and install the table.*** Attach the mounting block to the top end of the leg with #12 x 3″ flathead wood screws, then attach the mounting block to the underside of the table with #10 x 2″ screws. Also, attach the table cleat to the underside of the table with #10 x 2½″ screws. The back edge of the cleat should be flush with the back edge of the table.

Attach the cleat to the booth back with #10 x 1¼″ flathead wood screws. Do not glue the cleat to the booth back, in case you need to remove or replace the table at a later date.

9   ***Install the stiles and rails.*** Cut the stiles and rails to the proper length. Attach them to the booth back and bench backs with nails and glue. These strips help support the top trim and bench ends, and hide the seam between the plywood backs.

10   ***Make and install the bench ends.*** Enlarge the *Bench End Pattern* and trace it on the plywood stock. Cut the shapes with a saber saw or band saw, then sand the sawed edges. Cover the curved edges with veneer banding. Attach the bench ends to the bench assemblies with #10 x 1¼″ flathead wood screws. Counterbore and countersink the screws, then cover the heads.

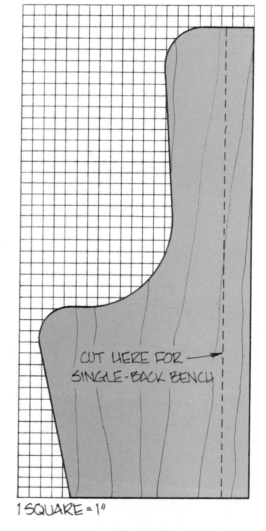

CUT HERE FOR
SINGLE-BACK BENCH

1 SQUARE = 1″

**BENCH END
PATTERN**

11   ***Install the trim and moldings.*** Using a table-mounted router and a ½″ cove bit, cut a cove in the edge of a ¾″-thick board. For safety, this board should be at least 3″ wide. Rip a ¾″-wide strip from the shaped edge of the board to make the cove molding. Cut the molding to length and attach it to the booth back with glue and nails. The top edge of the molding should be flush with the top edge of the plywood back.

Miter the top trim as shown in the *Top View,* and attach it to the top edges of the bench ends, bench backs, and booth back with nails and glue.

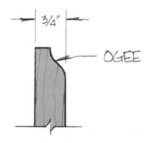

¾″

OGEE

BASE MOLDING DETAIL

Using a table-mounted router and an ogee bit, cut a decorative edge in the base molding and wall moldings. Miter the ends of the base molding at 78° and attach it to the booth back, between the two bench assemblies. Cut the wall moldings to length and miter the *ogee* portions *only,* so they fit together as shown in the *Wall Molding Assembly Detail.* Attach the wall moldings to the plywood booth wall with nails and glue.

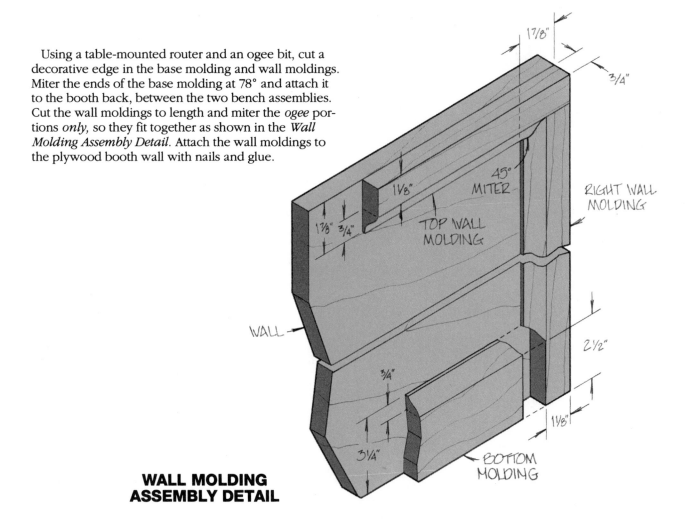

**WALL MOLDING
ASSEMBLY DETAIL**

---

12 **Finish the booth.** Lightly sand the surfaces of the booth. Be careful not to sand through the plywood veneer or the veneer banding. Apply paint, stain, and/or a clear finish to the wood surfaces.

Use a hard, waterproof paint or finish — one that will stand up to everyday use and abuse. Be careful not to get it on the laminated tabletop.

---

13 **Install cushions in the booth.** Cut 2"-thick pads of foam rubber to fit the bench seats and the bench backs. Sew a simple cloth case for each of these pads. Close one end of the case with a zipper or snaps so you can remove the pad easily to wash the upholstery.

Staple the "hook" sides of several Velcro fasteners to the bench backs and seats, and sew the "felt" sides to the bottoms or backs of the upholstered cushions. Place the cushions in the booth so the Velcro holds them securely.

TRY THIS! If you can't sew, take the foam pads to an upholstery shop and explain what you need. They will be able to cover the pads for you for a reasonable fee — this is a simple job for an experienced upholsterer.

Generic Table

In its most basic form, a table is a simple project. There are just three different parts — legs, aprons, and top. However, despite the simplicity of this form, you can create an infinite number of designs simply by changing the size or shape of the parts.

The table shown was built by Judy Ditmer, a professional woodturner and the proprietor of Heartwood in Tipp City, Ohio. She chose a contemporary design — a round top with square tapered legs. The top is about 3′ in diameter and 28″ off the floor; about

the right size and height to seat four people. Judy uses it for eating, working, and entertaining.

However, simply by enlarging the top to about 4′ in diameter, she could have had a formal dining table. By making the top smaller and shortening the legs slightly, she

could have had a side table or lamp stand. By elongating the top and shortening the legs to bring the top just 16″ to 18″ off the floor, Judy might have built a coffee table. And all of those tables would have exactly the same number of parts and identical joinery.

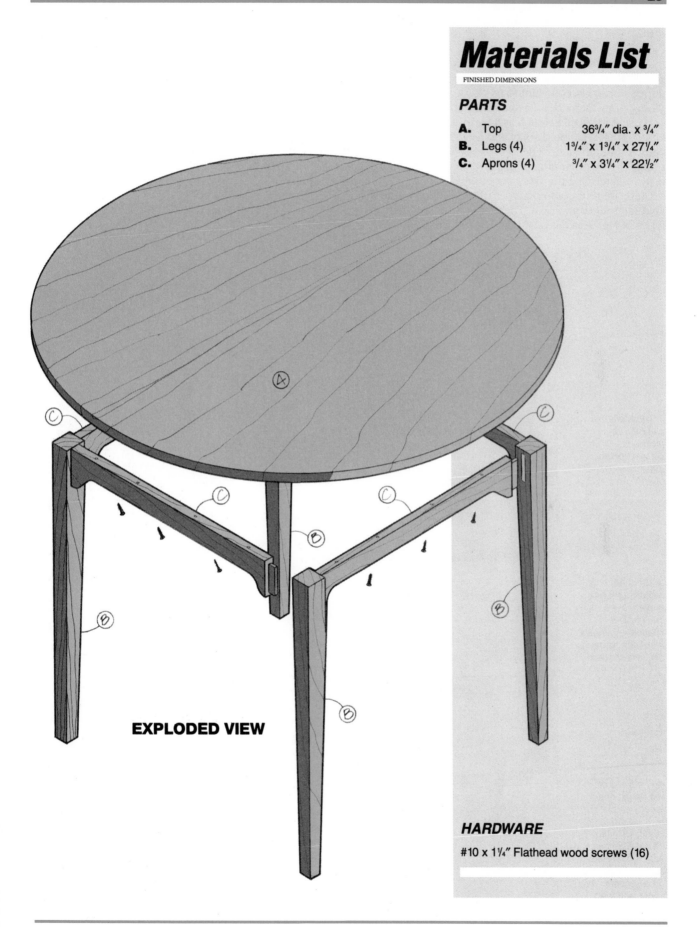

Materials List

FINISHED DIMENSIONS

PARTS

A. Top $36^{3}/_{4}''$ dia. x $^{3}/_{4}''$
B. Legs (4) $1^{3}/_{4}''$ x $1^{3}/_{4}''$ x $27^{1}/_{4}''$
C. Aprons (4) $^{3}/_{4}''$ x $3^{1}/_{4}''$ x $22^{1}/_{2}''$

EXPLODED VIEW

HARDWARE

#10 x $1^{1}/_{4}''$ Flathead wood screws (16)

1

Decide on the size and design of the table. The size of the table you build will depend on what you want to use it for. If you use it for dining, how many people should be able to sit at it? If you use it for display (such as a lamp stand or a coffee table), what will you display and how high do you want to hold the items? Refer to Table and Chair Ergonomics at the beginning of this book for suggestions on how to determine the size of your table.

There are four common types of tops — square, rectangular, round, and oval. There are also four common types of legs — straight, tapered, turned, and cabriole.

Aprons are either straight or shaped. (See Figures 1, 2, and 3.) Within each of these types there are many, many variations. For example, you can choose among several different styles of cabriole legs. And there are an infinite number of shapes that you can create when cutting an apron. Figure 4 shows how various combinations of parts can create four very different designs.

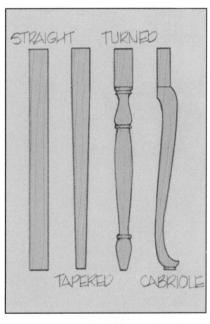

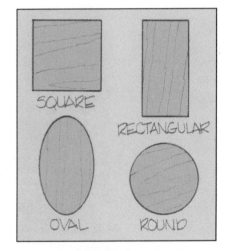

1/There are four common types of tabletops — square, rectangular, round, and oval.

2/There are four common types of table legs — straight, tapered, turned, and cabriole.

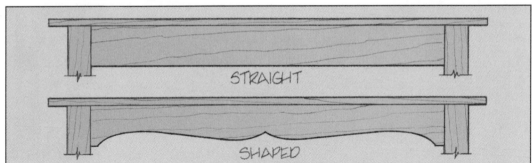

3/There are only two different types of aprons — straight and shaped — although there can be many different shapes.

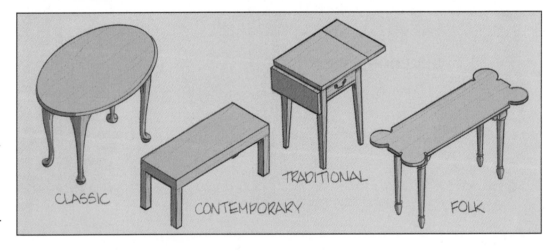

4/The types of tops, legs, and aprons can be combined to create a variety of table designs. Shown here are four possibilities — classic, contemporary, traditional, and folk.

2

Select the stock and cut the parts to size. When you have designed your table, select the stock for it. You can use almost any type of cabinet-grade wood, although you'll find that as a general rule, hardwoods wear better than softwoods — they're stronger, more durable, and resist dents and scratches. Make sure the stock for the legs is relatively clear, straight, and free of defects. To make the contemporary round table shown, you'll need about 14 board feet of 4/4 (four-quarters) stock, and 4 board feet of 8/4 (eight-quarters) stock. If you've changed the size or the design, you may need more or less of each.

Plane the 4/4 stock to ¾" thick and glue up the boards needed to make the wide tabletop. Cut the top and aprons to the widths and lengths needed. Rip and plane the 8/4 stock to make four square legs. (See Figures 5, 6, and 7.)

TRY THIS! When you glue up the wood for the tabletop, make sure the annual growth rings all cup *up* as you look at the end grain. If some of the rings cup up and the others cup down, the top may become "wavy" as the wood ages. If the rings all cup down, the edges will want to curl up. If the rings cup up, the wood will tend to rise in the center, but you can easily control this tendency with a few well-placed screws.

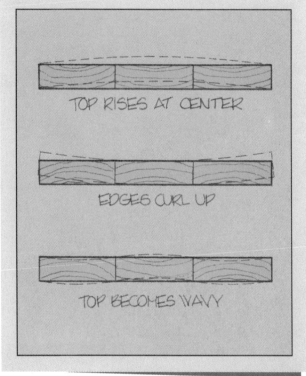

5/To make perfectly straight square legs, rip them from the rough stock **before** you plane it. These rough legs should be as wide as the stock is thick. For example, if you're ripping 8/4 stock, the rough legs should be 2" wide.

6/Joint two adjacent sides of the leg stock so the sides are perfectly flat and precisely 90° from each other. Mark the jointed sides with a pencil.

7/Plane the leg stock to its finished size, removing stock from the two sides that you did not joint. Set the planer depth of cut; run the board through once; turn it 90° and run it through again. Repeat until the legs are the proper thickness and width. Be careful not to remove the pencil marks as you plane.

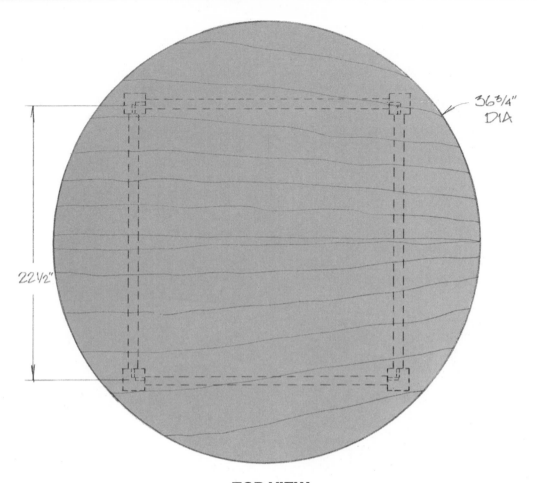

36 3/4" DIA

22 1/2"

TOP VIEW

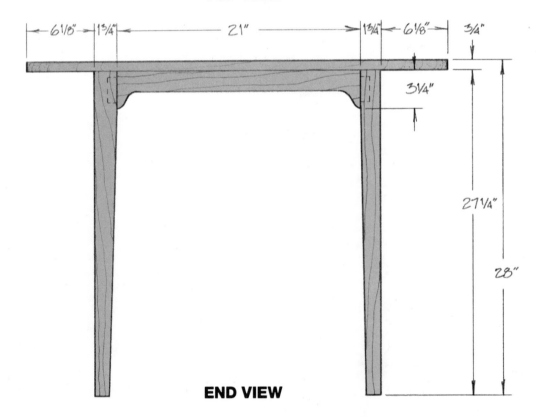

6 1/8" — 1 3/4" — 21" — 1 3/4" — 6 1/8" — 3/4"

3 1/4"

27 1/4"

28"

END VIEW

3 **Cut the mortises and tenons.** Traditionally, the ends of the aprons are tenoned. These tenons fit in mortises near the upper ends of the legs. Cut the mortises first, then fit the tenons to them. (See Figures 8 through 13.)

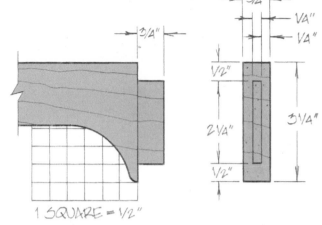

FRONT VIEW   **SIDE VIEW**

APRON DETAIL

1 SQUARE = 1/2"

*8/*Mark the mortises on the **inside** surfaces of each leg with a marking gauge or scratch awl. In addition to marking the perimeter of each mortise, score a line down the center.

*9/*Drill a line of overlapping holes to remove most of the stock from each mortise. Use a brad-point bit or similar self-centering bit. To line up the drill bit before drilling each hole, rest the point in the score mark you made down the center of the mortise. This will help keep the bit from wandering, so the rough mortise will be perfectly straight.

*10/*Clean up the edges and square the ends of the mortise with a chisel. If you have one, use a **mortising chisel.** These chisels are designed especially for this work.

*11/*Cut the tenons on the ends of the aprons with a dado cutter or table-mounted router. Using a miter gauge to guide the stock, pass the wood over the cutter or bit to make a rabbet along the end. Turn the stock over and cut another rabbet. The two rabbets will form a tenon.

12/Make your first tenon in a piece of scrap, then fit it to a mortise. If it's too loose, lower the bit or cutter slightly. If it's too tight, raise the setting. Cut another tenon and try again. When the scrap tenon fits properly, cut the tenons in the ends of the aprons.

13/To finish fitting the tenons to the mortises, cut the tenon shoulders with a dovetail saw or coping saw.

4 **Drill the screw pockets.** The top is held to the aprons with screws. Each screw rests in a *screw pocket* — a counterbore and pilot hole drilled at a slight angle to the inside face of the apron. Drill these pockets every 5"–10" along the length of the aprons. (See Figures 14 through 16.)

TRY THIS! Make the pilot holes in the screw pockets slightly larger than the shanks of the screws. For #10 screws, drill $7/32$"- or $1/4$"-diameter pilot holes. This will allow the top to expand and contract with changes in the weather — as the top moves, each screw will shift slightly in its pilot hole.

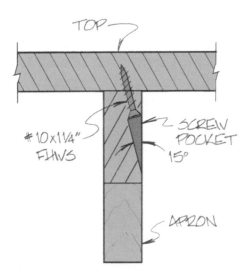

SCREW POCKET DETAIL

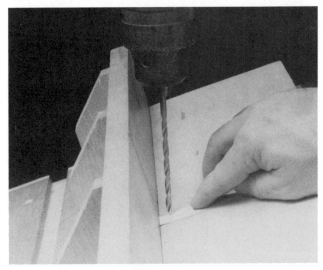

14/To drill a screw pocket, tilt the worktable of the drill press to 15°. Mount the **pilot hole** bit in the chuck and extend it until the bit touches the table. Clamp a fence to the **down** side of the table, about ⅜" away from the bit.

   Note: Before drilling the holes, lay down a large scrap of plywood or particleboard to prevent the bit from marring the table.

15/Remove the pilot hole bit from the chuck and replace it with the **counterbore** bit. Place the apron with the top edge down on the worktable and the outside face resting against the fence. Clamp the apron to the fence to keep it from shifting as you work. Drill the counterbore in the inside face, stopping about ½" above the table.
   Note: Use a Forstner bit to make the counterbores, if you have a set.

16/Remove the counterbore bit and replace it with the pilot hole bit. Do **not** loosen the clamp or shift the apron. Drill the pilot hole in the center of the counterbore, down through the apron. The bit should exit the wood approximately in the center of the top edge.

---

5 **Cut the shape of the top, if needed.** If you're making a round or oval tabletop, lay out the shape on the stock. Cut the shape with a band saw or a saber saw and sand the sawed edges. As you saw and sand, be particularly careful to preserve a "fair" curve — an even, graceful curved edge with no dips or high spots.

---

6 **Cut or turn the shape of the legs, if needed.** If you're making tapered legs, cut the tapers on a table saw using a tapering jig. Refer to Step-by-Step: Making Tapered Legs for more information. If you're making turned legs, turn them on a lathe. Use a storystick to help turn all four legs to the same shape. (See Figure 17.) If you're making cabriole legs, cut them on a band saw and sand the sawed surfaces. Refer to Step-by-Step: Making Cabriole Legs for more information.

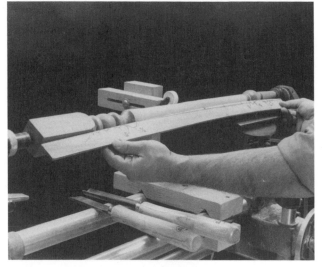

17/Before turning the leg, make a **storystick** — mark the shape of the leg and the diameters of the coves, beads, and flats on a long, slender scrap. Compare this storystick to the legs as you turn them.

7

Cut the shapes of the aprons, if needed.
If you're making shaped aprons, lay out the shapes on the stock. Cut the shapes with a band saw or scroll saw and sand the sawed edges.

TRY THIS!   If two or more aprons are the same size and shape, stick the stock together with double-faced carpet tape. Lay out the shape on the top piece in the stack, then cut and sand all the parts at the same time. This not only saves time, it ensures that all the aprons match precisely.

8

Assemble the table. Finish sand all the parts. (If you're making turned legs, finish sand these on the lathe.) Glue the apron tenon in the leg mortises, and clamp the parts together. Check that the aprons are square to one another as you tighten the clamps.

Let the glue dry completely and remove the clamps. Turn the top upside down on your workbench. Turn the leg-and-apron assembly upside down on the top. Center the assembly on the top, then clamp it in place. Drive flathead screws through the screw pockets and into the top. Tighten the screws so they're snug, but not overly tight. Do *not* glue the top to the aprons.

9

Finish the table. Do any necessary touch-up sanding, then apply a finish to the completed table. Be careful to apply as many coats to the underside of the table as you do the top — this will keep it from warping.

The best finish for the table will depend on how you intend to use it. For preparing food, dining, or entertaining, use a waterproof, washable finish such as polyurethane, spar varnish, or acrylic resin. For tables that may see a lot of heavy use — worktables, for example — use a penetrating oil finish, such as tung oil or Danish oil. These help to harden the surface of the wood and they're easy to renew if you happen to damage the tabletop. For formal tables, use ordinary varnish, lacquer, or shellac; these can be easily built up and buffed to take on the depth and luster you want.

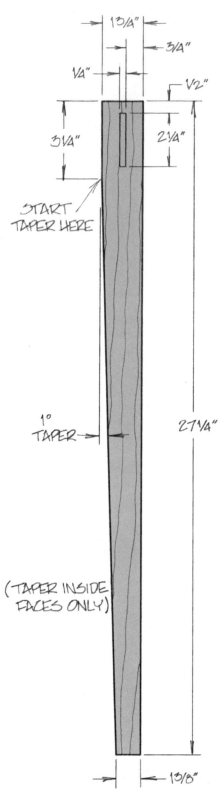

LEG LAYOUT

Step-by-Step: Making Tapered Legs

Some designers speculate that the appeal of tapered legs has deep, prehistoric roots. When our ancestors first began to build small structures from wooden posts, they turned the posts upside down so the *root* end (the *thick* end) was in the air. Perhaps the reason was superstitious — they may have believed that the dead tree would take root once again, begin to grow, and destroy the building. Perhaps it was practical — trees carry water much easier up a trunk than down it. With the poles root-end up, the wood remained drier and lasted longer.

Whatever the reason, woodworkers have been making supporting columns and legs that taper top to bottom for thousands of years. The tapers make these vertical members seem less heavy without detracting from their strength. This in turn adds grace and symmetry to the project

There are many different ways to make a tapered leg — you can use almost any saw to cut the taper. But perhaps the easiest and the most accurate way is to use a table saw and a tapering jig. If you don't have a jig, you can make one from a scrap of plywood.

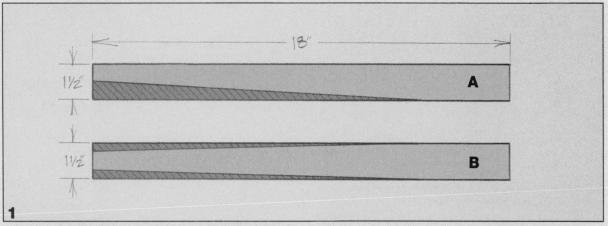

1

On a large piece of paper or poster board, draw a **full-size** profile of the leg blank. For example, if the leg is 1½" wide and 18" long, draw a rectangle 1½" by 18". Then draw the taper you want to cut on this rectangle, as shown on Leg A. If the leg tapers on both sides, as does Leg B, be sure to show this on the rectangle. The taper line(s) will form one or two right triangles on one or both sides of the rectangle.

2

Cut a scrap of plywood 2"–3" longer than the tapered section of the leg, and rip it 1"–2" wider than the leg. After ripping the stock for the jig, leave the fence in place — do **not** change the setting.

3

Place the leg drawing on the plywood and line up the taper line (or one of the taper lines) with one of the long edges of the board. The upper end of the taper line (where the leg starts to taper) should be over one of the upper corners of the board. Tape the drawing to the plywood.

(Continued)

Step-by-Step: Making Tapered Legs — Continued

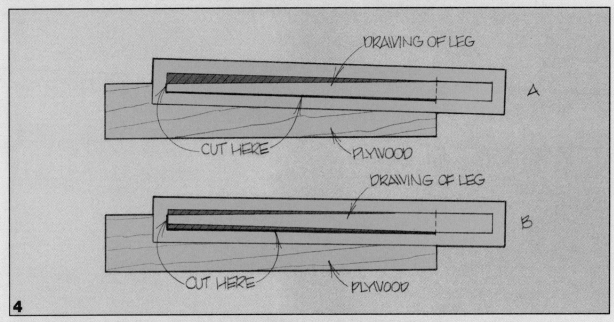

4

Using a band saw, saber saw, or hand saw, cut the plywood along the lines that mark the **untapered** side and bottom end of the leg. These are shown in bold on the drawing. If the leg is tapered on both sides, cut along the line that marks the straight side of the leg blank **before** you taper it.

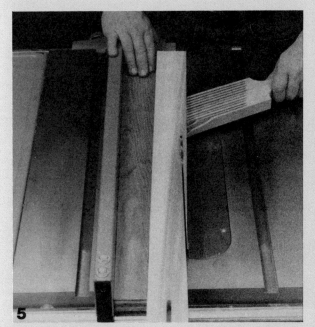

5

Place a leg blank in the plywood jig with the bottom end resting in the notch you just cut. Hold the straight edge of the jig against the table saw fence, turn the saw on, and slowly feed the jig and the leg past the blade. The saw will cut the taper **exactly** as you've drawn it. **(Saw guard removed for clarity.)**

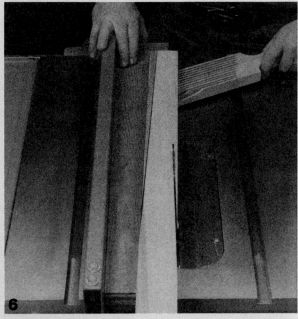

6

To make a second taper cut on the opposite side of the leg blank, save the scrap from the first cut. Use this as a spacer to hold the leg stock at the proper angle in the jig for the second cut. **(Saw guard removed for clarity.)**

Extension Table

Now and then, during holidays and celebrations, you may need a larger dining table than you have. There's no sense in keeping on hand a big table that you won't use but a few times each year. Fortunately, there are several ways to provide additional table space on special occasions without a bigger table. One of the simplest is to make an *extension* table — a medium-size table with an expandable top.

The tops of extension tables are split so you can pull them apart and add leaves between the halves. Normally, the halves are joined with special "slides" — telescoping aprons. These slides also support the additional leaves. When you no longer need the full table space, remove the leaves and slide the table halves back together.

The extension table shown, built by Larry Callahan of West Milton, Ohio, is typical of many. In normal everyday use, without the leaves, it will accommodate 4 to 6 people. With one 15"-wide leaf installed, 6 to 8 people can use it. And with both leaves in place, it will seat up to 10 people.

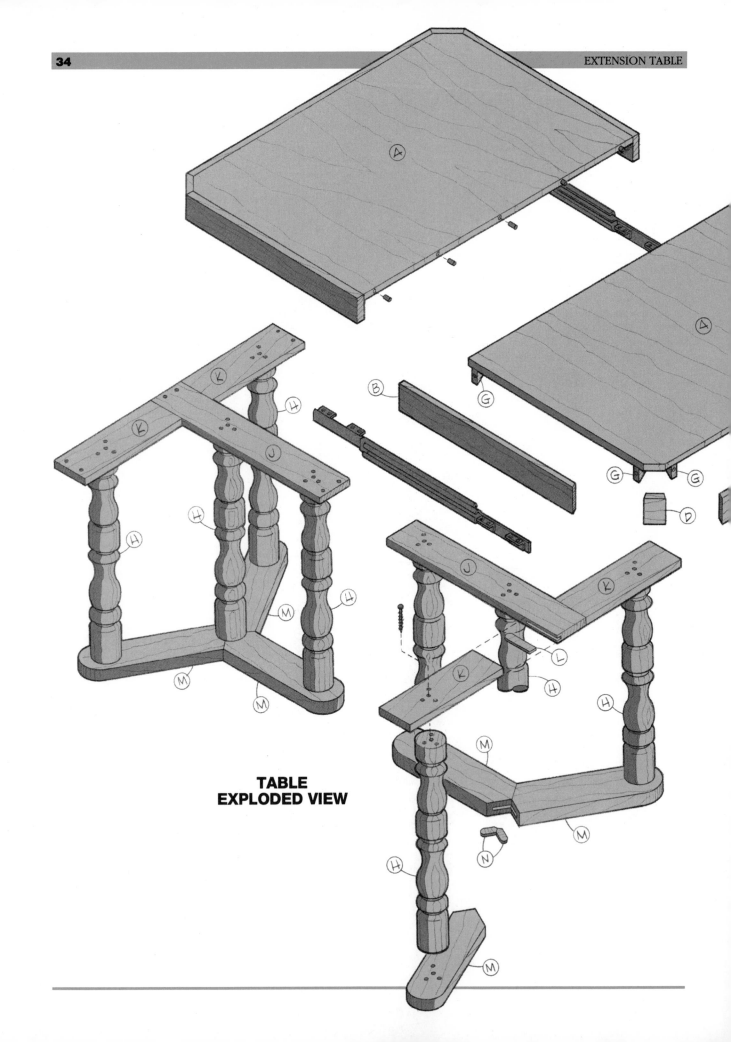

**TABLE
EXPLODED VIEW**

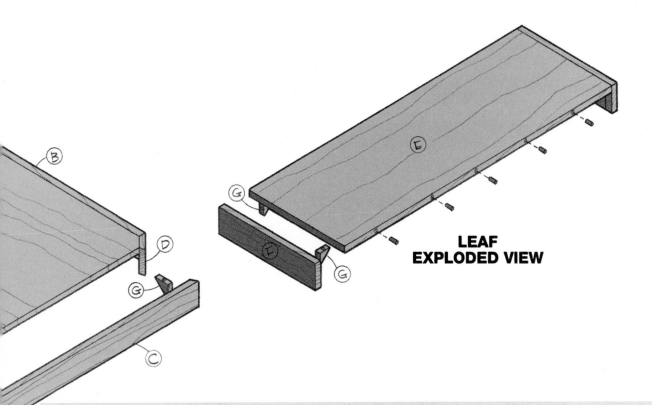

**LEAF
EXPLODED VIEW**

Materials List

FINISHED DIMENSIONS

PARTS

A.	Top halves* (2)	³/₄″ x 29⁷/₈″ x 43½″
B.	Side trim (4)	³/₄″ x 3¼″ x 28⅛″
C.	End trim (2)	³/₄″ x 3¼″ x 40″
D.	Corner trim (4)	³/₄″ x 3¼″ x 3½″
E.	Leaves* (2)	³/₄″ x 15″ x 43½″
F.	Leaf trim (4)	³/₄″ x 3¼″ x 15″
G.	Glue blocks (20)	³/₄″ x 2⅛″ x 2⅛″
H.	Legs (8)	3½″ dia. x 27″

J.	Long top cleats (2)	³/₄″ x 4¾″ x 27″
K.	Short top cleats (4)	³/₄″ x 4¾″ x 15½″
L.	Cleat splines* (4)	¼″ x 1″ x 4¾″
M.	Feet (6)	1½″ x 4½″ x 18⅛″
N.	Feet splines* (6)	¼″ x 1″ x 2⅛″

Make these parts from plywood.

HARDWARE

36″ Extension slides and mounting screws (2)

¼″ dia. x 1″ Brass pins (15)

#12 x 3″ Flathead wood screws (48)

#12 x 1¼″ Flathead wood screws (16)

#10 x 1¼″ Flathead wood screws (40)

---

1 **Select the stock and cut the parts to size.** To make this project, you need about 15 board feet of 4/4 (four-quarters) stock, 9 board feet of 8/4 (eight-quarters) stock, one 4′ x 8′ sheet of cabinet-grade plywood, a scrap of ¼″ plywood, and eight 3½″ x 3½″ x 30″ turning squares. You can use almost any cabinet-grade wood and matching plywood; however, hardwoods will wear better. The table shown is made from oak and oak-veneer plywood.

After selecting the wood, plane the 4/4 stock to ¾″ thick, and the 8/4 stock to 1½″ thick. Cut all the parts to the sizes shown in the Materials List, except the feet — make these about 2″ longer than specified. Make the tabletop halves and leaves from ¾″ plywood, the splines from ¼″ plywood, and the remaining parts from solid wood. To make the glue blocks, cut 10 squares, ¾″ x 2⅛″ x 2⅛″. Then split these squares diagonally on a band saw to make 20 triangular blocks.

2 **Turn the legs.** Turn the legs on a lathe. You can turn them to the shape shown in the *Leg Layout,* or design your own legs. Match all eight legs as closely as possible. If you have a duplicating lathe, use it to copy the legs. If not, make a *storystick* to help lay out and measure each leg. (See Figure 1.) On this storystick, draw a full-size profile of the leg shape. Also, indicate the diameters of the beads and flats (major diameters) and the coves and troughs (minor diameters).

Round the leg stock. Using the storystick, mark the locations of the beads, coves, and other shapes on the legs. Turn the major and minor diameters, making a series of grooves in each spindle with a parting tool.

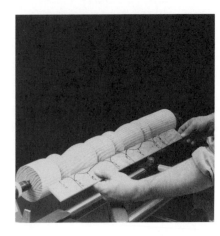

1/To help duplicate the leg turnings, make a storystick that shows the shape and dimensions of the leg. Use this storystick to mark the locations of the beads and coves, then compare it to the turning now and then as you work.

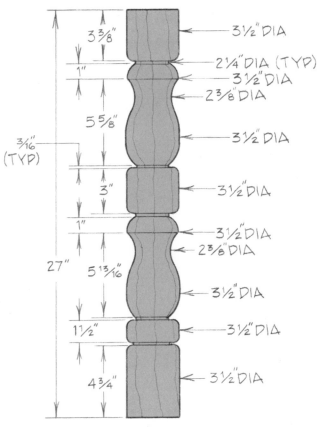

LEG LAYOUT

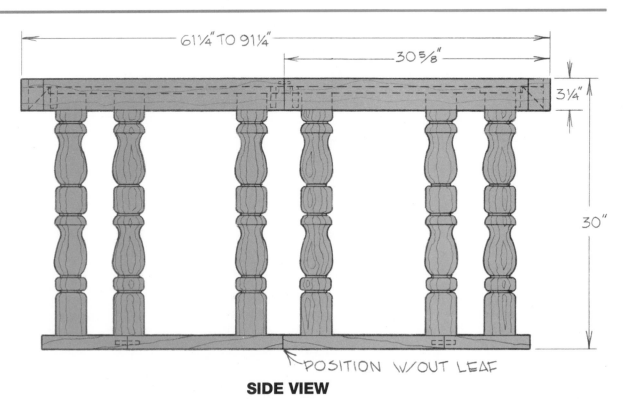

SIDE VIEW

Gauge the diameters at the bottom of these grooves with calipers.

Turn the beads first, then the coves, working from major to minor diameters. As the spindle takes shape on the lathe, check your progress now and then with the storystick. Compare the shapes on the pattern with those in the wood, and try to match them as closely as possible. When you've completed each leg, finish sand it on the lathe.

3 **Cut the shapes of the feet.** The "inside" ends of the feet are double-mitered to fit together. Cut these special miters on a table saw or radial arm saw. Set the saw to cut a 60° angle, and make one pass across the end of the stock. Attach a stop block to the backstop or miter gauge to help position the stock for the second pass. Turn the stock over and make the second miter cut, creating a point on the end of the stock. (See Figure 2.) This point must be perfectly centered side to side on the stock, and the mitered surfaces must be exactly 120° apart.

2/To help position the leg stock on the saw for the second miter cut, attach a stop block to the miter gauge (if you're using a table saw) or the backstop (if you're using a radial arm saw). Butt the mitered end of the stock against the block, then make the second pass. This will create a point on the end of the stock.

TRY THIS! Double-miter three test pieces first, to see if the saw angle is properly set. If the parts gap in the center when you put them together, the angle is too large. If they gap at the edges of the boards, it's too small. Adjust the miter gauge or radial arm accordingly.

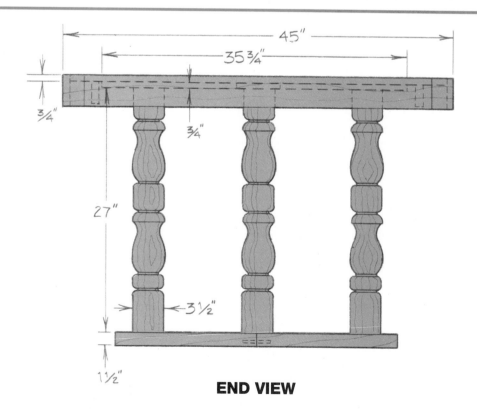

END VIEW

When you've double-mitered the feet, arrange them in two stacks of three boards each, with the mitered ends flush. Stick the stacks together with double-faced carpet tape. Lay out the rounded ends on the top boards in each stack, as shown in the *Feet Layout*. Cut the rounded ends on a band saw, then sand the sawed edges, sawing and sanding three legs at once. Disassemble the stacks and discard the tape.

4 *Cut the splines and spline grooves.*

The cleats are joined end to edge to make two T-shaped assemblies, and the mitered ends of the feet are joined to create two Y-shaped assemblies. The joints of all four assemblies are reinforced with ¼"-thick, 1"-wide splines. These splines rest in ¼"-wide, ½"-deep grooves.

Cut the spline grooves with a table-mounted router and a spline cutter. Use a fence to guide the boards when making the grooves in the edges of the long cleats. Attach a stop block to the fence to stop each groove when it's 4¾" long. (See Figure 3.) Cut the grooves in the ends of the short cleats and feet, using the miter gauge to guide the boards. Mark the mitered ends of the feet where you want to halt the spline groove, and stop cutting when you reach the mark. (See Figure 4.)

After cutting the grooves, shape the splines to fit them. Round one end of each cleat spline, as shown in the *Cleat Spline Layout*. Round one end of each foot spline in the same manner, then double-miter the other end, as shown in the *Foot Spline Layout*.

3/When cutting the spline grooves in the long cleats, use a fence to guide the work. Attach a stop block to the fence to halt the cut when the groove is long enough.

4/To cut the grooves in the short cleats and feet, use a miter gauge to guide the work. When cutting the mitered ends of the feet, halt the groove before you break through the edge of the stock.

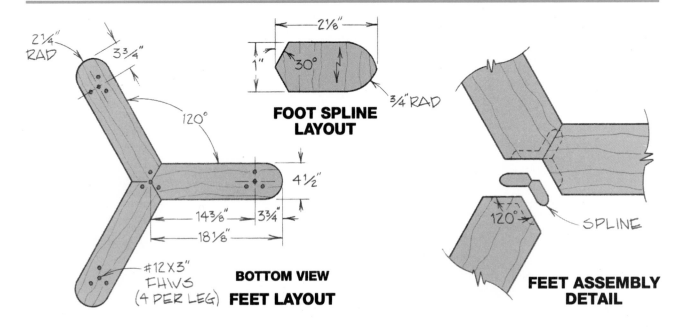

2¼" RAD

3¾"

120°

14⅜"   3¾"

18⅛"

4½"

#12 X 3" FHWS (4 PER LEG)

BOTTOM VIEW
FEET LAYOUT

2⅛"

1"   30°

¾" RAD

FOOT SPLINE LAYOUT

120°

SPLINE

FEET ASSEMBLY DETAIL

5

Assemble the bases. Finish sand the feet, and lightly sand the cleats. Glue the long and short cleats together end to edge, as shown in the *Cleat Layout/Top View,* slipping the splines into the grooves. Also, glue the feet together end to end, as shown in the *Feet Layout/Bottom View.*

When the glue dries, assemble the cleats, feet, and legs to make two bases. (Each base consists of one T-shaped cleat assembly, one Y-shaped feet assembly, and four legs.) Glue the ends of the legs to the feet and cleats, then reinforce the joints with #12 x 3" flathead wood screws.

6

Install the leveling pins in the top halves and leaves. The inside edge of one top half is fitted with brass leveling pins, and the other has matching holes. When the two halves are pushed together, these pins rest in the holes. The leaves also have matching pins and holes in the edges. This arrangement keeps the tabletop level.

To install these pins, put the top halves together, inside edge to inside edge. Label the right and left halves, then mark the locations of the pins and holes on both boards, marking across the seam. Drill 1/4"-diameter, 1/2"-deep holes at the marks, centered in the edges. Use a doweling jig to guide the drill.

Pull the halves apart and put a leaf between them. Mark the right and left edges of the leaf. Transfer the marks on the edges of the halves to the edges of the leaves. Repeat for the second leaf. Drill holes in the edges of the leaves, using the doweling jig.

Install 1/4"-diameter, 1"-long brass pins in the holes in the inside edge of the *left* top half and the *left* edges of the leaves. Secure the pins with epoxy.

When the epoxy sets, test the fit of the top halves and leaves. The pins should fit in the holes without having to be forced. When the top halves and leaves are pushed together, the top surfaces and side edges should be flush.

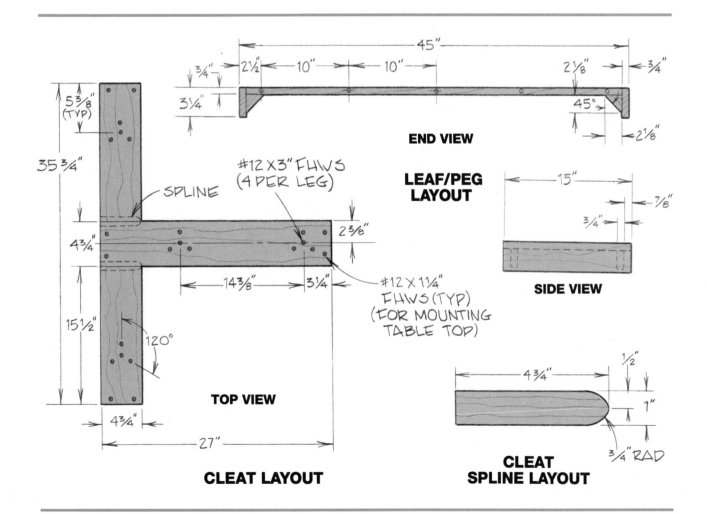

END VIEW

LEAF/PEG LAYOUT

SIDE VIEW

TOP VIEW

CLEAT LAYOUT

CLEAT SPLINE LAYOUT

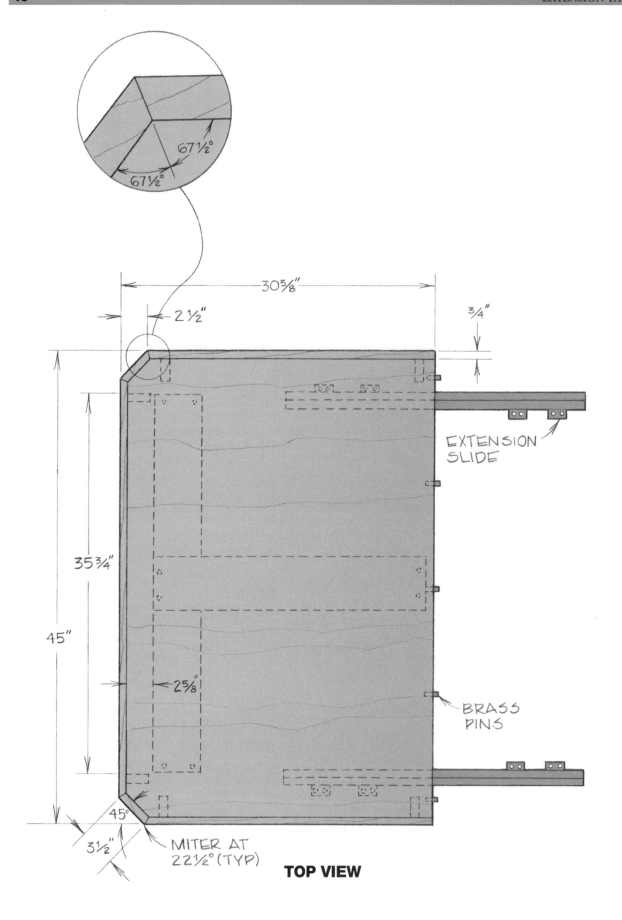

67½°

67½°

30⅝"

2½"

¾"

EXTENSION
SLIDE

35¾"

45"

2⅝"

BRASS
PINS

45°

3½"

MITER AT
22½° (TYP)

TOP VIEW

7 **Trim the top halves and the leaves.** The plywood top halves and leaves are edged with 3¼"-wide solid wood trim. This not only hides the plies, it makes the top look more substantial without adding unnecessary weight.

Miter the corners of the top halves at 45°, as shown in the *Top View*. Also miter the adjoining ends of the side trim, end trim, and corner trim at 22½°. Glue the trim to the outside edges of the top halves and leaves.

Drill counterbores and pilot holes in the diagonal edges of the glue blocks, as shown in the *Glue Block Assembly Detail*. (See Figure 5.) Glue the blocks to the underside of the top halves, against the trim. Reinforce them with #10 x 1¼" flathead wood screws.

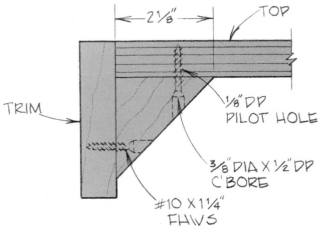

**GLUE BLOCK
ASSEMBLY DETAIL**

5/Drill the pilot holes in the diagonal edges of the glue blocks on the drill press. Make a simple jig from scrap wood to position the blocks under the bit and hold them steady.

8 **Attach the top halves to the bases.** Turn the top halves upside down on your workbench, inside edge to inside edge. Push them together so the pins in the left half mate with the holes in the right. Turn the bases upside down and center them on the top halves. Mark their positions and remove them.

Mount two 36" extension slides to the underside of the top halves, following the manufacturer's directions. Make sure the slides are *collapsed* when you install them. Also make sure they clear the marks for the bases.

Replace the bases on the top. Drill and countersink pilot holes through the cleats and into the top halves. Be careful not to drill through the top surface. Then attach the base assemblies to the top assembly with #12 x 1¼" flathead wood screws.

9 **Finish the table.** Have an assistant help you turn the table right side up. Test the action of the extension slides. Pull the top halves apart, then push them back together again. Add one leaf, then two leaves, then take them apart again.

When you're satisfied the extension slides work and the leaves fit properly, put the table together with two leaves. Finish sand the top halves, leaves, and trim. Be careful not to remove too much stock from the plywood parts — you don't want to sand through the veneer. Also, do any necessary touch-up sanding of the base assemblies.

Remove the leaves and the extension slides from the table. Apply a durable, waterproof finish, such as spar varnish or polyurethane, to all the wood surfaces. When the finish dries, rub it out and buff it with one or two coats of paste wax. Replace the slides and push the top halves together.

Cottage Rocker

During the Victorian era, furnituremakers began making "cottage" furniture — rustic pieces based on traditional country designs. These designs were adapted, however, so they could be produced by machine rather than hand. This didn't necessarily cheapen the piece, making it less attractive or less durable, but simply made it easier to produce.

The rocker shown is a good example. The design is adapted from a traditional Windsor rocker. Yet it requires little handwork; there are no spindles to bend and you cut the seat shape on the band saw. Most of the curved parts are cut on a band saw, then rounded over. The lathe work, too, has been kept to a minimum. Only the front and back rungs are turned. The other spindles are shaped with a spokeshave or a plane, and the tenons are cut on a drill press. Yet for all this machine work, the rocker is strong and durable, and displays the same graceful lines as a traditional Windsor piece.

Materials List

FINISHED DIMENSIONS

PARTS

A.	Seat	1³/₄" x 17³/₄" x 18"
B.	Front legs (2)	1¹/₂" x 1¹/₂" x 14"
C.	Back legs (2)	1¹/₂" x 1¹/₂" x 13³/₄"
D.	Rockers (2)	³/₄" x 4⁷/₈" x 27"
E.	Front rung	1¹/₄" dia. x 15⁷/₈"
F.	Back rung	1¹/₄" dia. x 12³/₄"
G.	Side rungs (2)	1" x 2¹/₂" x 16"
H.	Front brace	1³/₄" x 1³/₄" x 17³/₄"
J.	Back brace	1³/₄" x 3¹/₈" x 13¹/₂"
K.	Arms (2)	1" x 4" x 17¹/₂"
L.	Arm supports (2)	1" x 2³/₈" x 21¹/₂"
M.	Back posts (2)	1" x 2¹/₈" x 27"
N.	Spindles (4)	³/₄" x ³/₄" x 21¹/₂"
P.	Headrest	2" x 7³/₄" x 15¹/₂"
Q.	Rocker dowels (4)	¹/₂" dia. x 1¹/₂"
R.	Arm support dowels (2)	¹/₂" dia. x 3"
S.	Headrest dowels (4)	¹/₂" dia. x 1¹/₂"
T.	Leg wedges (4)	³/₃₂" x 1" x 1¹/₄"
U.	Arm support wedges (2)	³/₃₂" x ³/₄" x ⁷/₈"

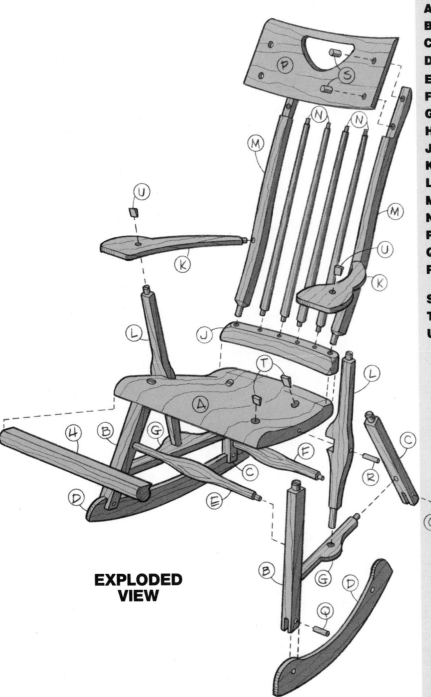

EXPLODED VIEW

HARDWARE

#10 x 2¹/₂" Flathead wood screws (6)

1 Select the stock and cut the parts to size.

Select the stock and cut the parts to size. To make this project, you need about 4 board feet of 4/4 (four-quarters) stock, 20 board feet of 8/4 (eight-quarters) stock, and a ½″-diameter, 14″-long dowel. You can make this rocker from almost any cabinet-grade wood; however, you should use a hardwood with clear, straight grain for the long, slender parts, such as the legs, rungs, back posts, and spindles. Windsor chairs were traditionally constructed from several species of domestic American woods. The seats were often made from pine or poplar, the turned parts from maple, birch, or oak, and the curved parts from hickory, ash, or chestnut. The rocker shown is made entirely from maple.

When you have selected the wood, plane the 4/4 stock to ¾″ thick. Cut the rockers to the sizes specified in the Materials List, and cut the spindles about 1″ longer than shown.

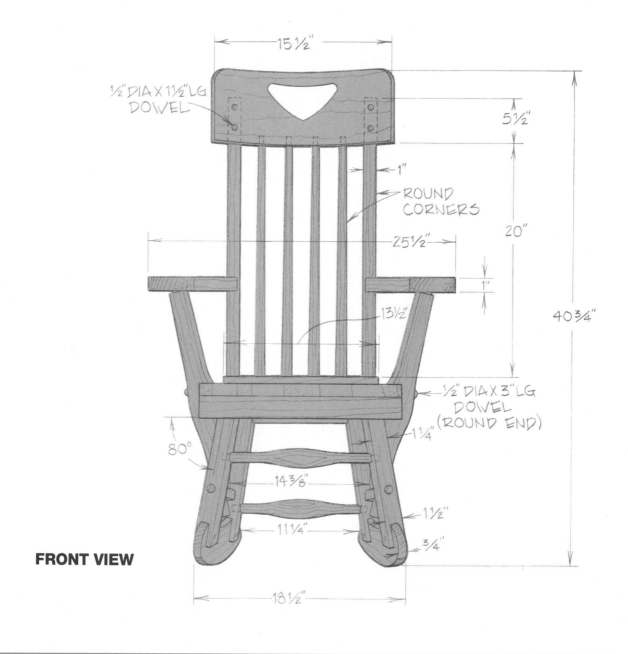

FRONT VIEW

Plane the 8/4 stock to 1¾″ thick and cut the seat, braces, and headrest. Make the seat from two or three boards, no wider than your band saw's depth of cut. For instance, if your band saw has a 6″ depth of cut, cut three boards for the seat, each 6″ wide and 18″ long. This will allow you to cut the seat scoop on your band saw. Do *not* glue the seat boards together yet.

Do the same for the headrest. If the band saw depth of cut is less than 7¾″, make the headrest from two

4″-wide, 15½″-long boards. Do *not* glue the parts together; wait until after you've cut their shape.

After cutting all the 1¾″-thick parts, plane the remaining stock to 1½″ and cut the legs. Also cut turning squares for the front and back rungs — make these rung blanks about 1″ longer than specified. Resaw and plane the remaining 1½″-thick stock to 1″ and cut the side rungs, arms, arm supports, and back posts. Once again, make the rungs about 1″ longer than shown.

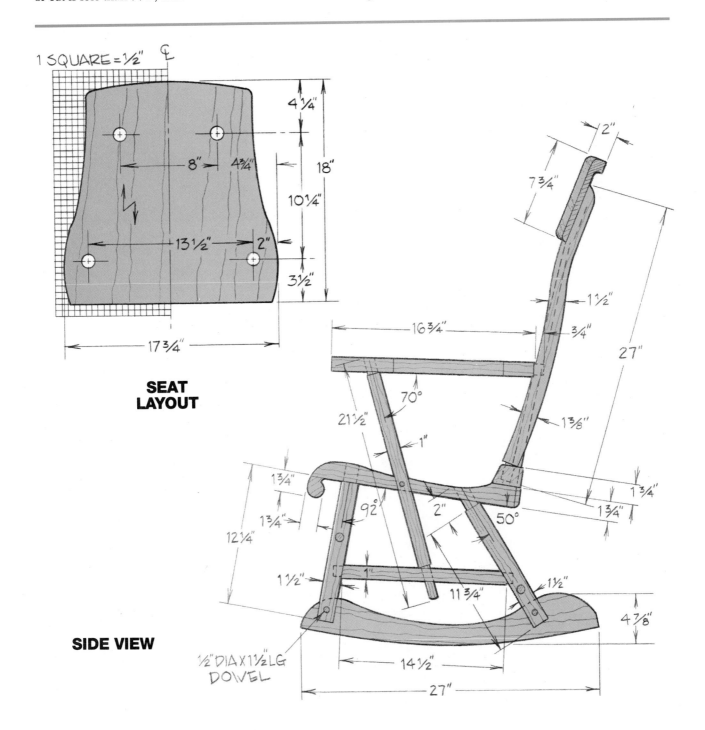

SEAT LAYOUT

SIDE VIEW

2 Make the seat. Windsor chair construction always starts with the seat, and this rocker is no different. Temporarily dry clamp the seat boards together, edge to edge, with the bottom side facing up. Lay out the shape of the seat and the location of the round leg mortises on the stock. Using a hand-held power drill and a 1″ spade bit, drill the round mortises. Use a simple *Drill Guide* to help gauge the compound angles.

Don't worry if you don't drill the leg mortises at the precise angles indicated on the *Front View* and *Side View*. It won't matter if they're a few degrees off. Also, don't be overly concerned if there's some tear-out where the drill bit exits the seat stock — you'll cut away the torn stock when you saw the seat profile.

Enlarge the *Seat Profile Pattern* and trace it onto the edges of the seat boards. Using the band saw, cut the profile in each board, then glue them together edge to edge. Do *not* sand the surface of the seat yet.

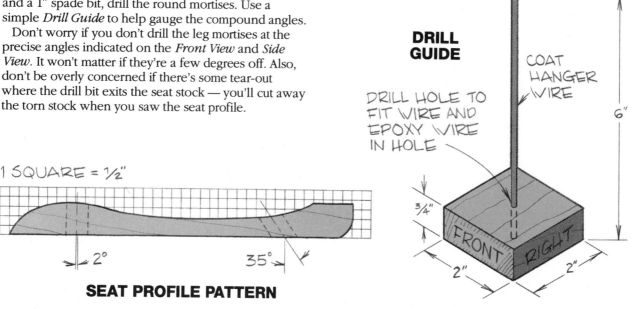

1 SQUARE = ½″

2°   35°

SEAT PROFILE PATTERN

DRILL GUIDE

COAT HANGER WIRE

DRILL HOLE TO FIT WIRE AND EPOXY WIRE IN HOLE

6″   ¾″   2″   2″

FRONT   RIGHT

3 Cut and fit the legs. Lay out the tapers and slots on the legs, as shown in the *Front Leg Layout* and *Back Leg Layout*. Cut the tapers and slots on a band saw, then sand the sawed edges. "Break" the corners of the legs with a rasp and file, rounding them slightly. Measure and mark the locations of the round mortises for the rungs, but don't drill them yet.

Cut the tenons in the top ends of the legs on a drill press, using a tenon cutter. (See Figure 1.) Fit the legs to the seat and, using the ¾″-thick rocker stock as a guide, turn the legs so the slots line up. Mark the slots for the wedges on the protruding ends of the tenons — these slots should be perpendicular to the grain direction of the seat.

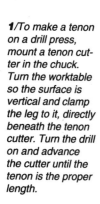

1/To make a tenon on a drill press, mount a tenon cutter in the chuck. Turn the worktable so the surface is vertical and clamp the leg to it, directly beneath the tenon cutter. Turn the drill on and advance the cutter until the tenon is the proper length.

2/To make the round rung mortises in a leg, clamp the leg to the work-bench, near the edge, so the out-side surface faces up. Mount a spade bit in a hand-held power drill, and put the point of the bit where you want to drill the mortise. Line up the shaft of the bit with the mark on the leg that indicates the angle of the mortise, then drill the mortise.

Measure the distances between the marks you've made for the rung mortises. (If any of these distances are different from what is shown on the *Front View* or *Side View,* you'll have to adjust the length of the rungs accordingly.) Using a straightedge, draw a line on the outside face of each leg that indicates the angle of these mortises. Remove the legs from the seat and drill the rung mortises, using the lines to help gauge the angle. (See Figure 2.)

4 **Cut or turn the shapes of the rungs and rockers.** If necessary, adjust the length of the rungs and trim the stock to the proper length. Enlarge the *Side Rung Layout and Pattern*. Trace it onto the stock, and mark the locations of the round mortises for the arm supports. However, don't drill these holes yet. Also enlarge the *Rocker Pattern* and trace it onto the wood. Cut the shapes on a band saw, then sand the sawed edges. Round over the edges of the side rungs with a router or shaper, using a 1/2″ quarter-round bit or cutter. Do *not* round the edges of the rockers yet.

Cut the tenons in all the rungs and rung blanks on a drill press, using the same method you used for the legs. Turn the front and back rungs to the shapes shown in the *Front Rung Layout* and *Back Rung Layout*. Finish sand these rungs on the lathe.

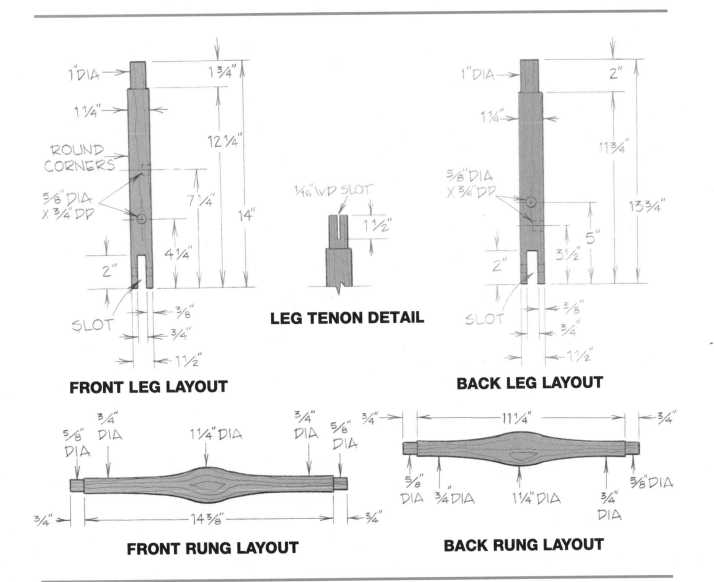

FRONT LEG LAYOUT

LEG TENON DETAIL

BACK LEG LAYOUT

FRONT RUNG LAYOUT

BACK RUNG LAYOUT

5 **Cut the shapes of the front brace.** Drill and counterbore three pilot holes through the front brace stock, as shown in the *Brace Joinery Detail*. The precise location of these holes is not critical, but they should be evenly spaced along the length of the brace. Cut a V-shaped groove in the back edge on a table saw, then round over the front edge with a jack plane, as shown in the *Front Brace Profile*.

6 **Assemble the seat, front brace, legs, rungs, and rockers.** Finish sand all the parts you've made so far *except* the top surface of the seat. Dry assemble the seat, legs, rungs, and rockers to make sure they fit together properly. Disassemble them and glue the rungs to the legs. Before the glue dries, glue the legs in the seat and the rockers to the legs.

From scrap stock, cut four wedges and tap them into the slots in the tops of the legs. Also, cut four ½″-diameter, 1½″-long dowels. Drill ½″-diameter holes through the legs and rockers, near the bottom ends, as shown in the *Side View*. Glue the dowels in these holes.

Using a dovetail saw or coping saw, cut off the leg tenons flush with the top surface of the seat. Attach the front brace to the bottom of the seat, flush with the front edge, using flathead wood screws. Do *not* glue the brace to the seat. Finish sand the top surface of the seat and blend the front edge with the brace so the seat "rolls" at the front.

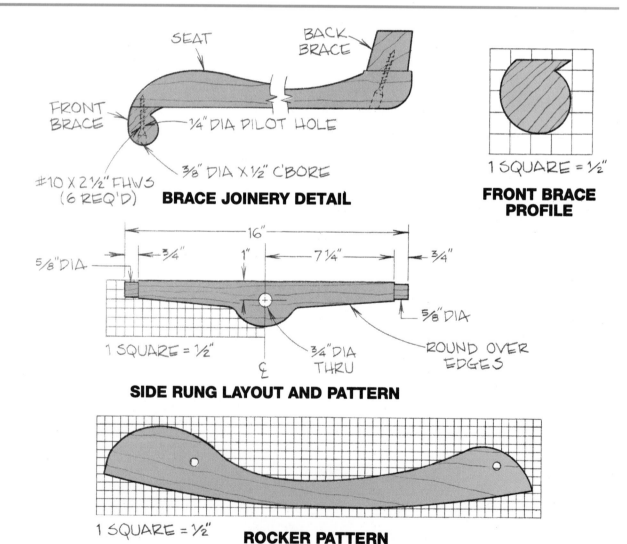

BRACE JOINERY DETAIL

FRONT BRACE PROFILE

SIDE RUNG LAYOUT AND PATTERN

ROCKER PATTERN

7

Drill the mortises in the back brace and headrest. Enlarge the patterns in the *Back Brace Layout* and *Headrest Layout*. Trace these onto the stock, and mark the locations of the round mortises for the back posts and spindles.

Drill the spindle mortises in the bottom edge of the headrest stock. Tilt the drill press table at 7°, and drill the spindle mortises and back post mortises in the top edge of the back brace stock.

8

Cut the shapes of the back brace, headrest, and back posts. Enlarge the *Back Post Pattern* and trace it onto the stock. Cut the tenons on the bottom ends of the posts with a drill press, then cut the shape of the posts with a band saw.

Make the cutout in the headrest with a scroll saw, saber saw, or — if you're making the headrest in two parts — a band saw. Then cut the curve of the headrest on a band saw. If necessary, glue the headrest boards together edge to edge. (See Figures 3 and 4.)

Tilt the band saw table to 7° and saw the back edge of the back brace. Increase the tilt to 20° and saw the front edge. Sand the sawed edges and faces of the back brace, headrest, and back posts, *except* the front surface of the headrest.

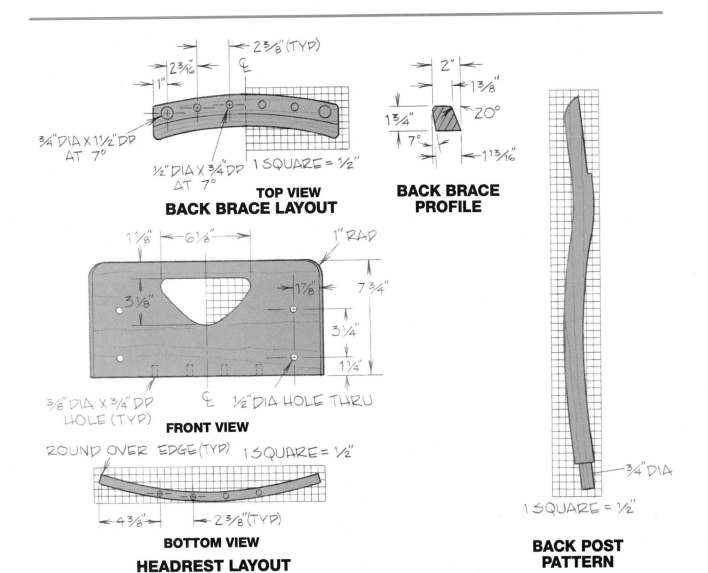

3/To shape the headrest boards, first saw the cutout, removing waste from each board. Then cut the curve in the edge of both boards.

4/Glue the headrest boards edge to edge. When the boards are joined, the cutout should become a closed, half-moon-shaped hole.

9 **Make the spindles.** Temporarily dry assemble the back brace, back posts, and headrest. Measure the distance between the back brace and the headrest. If the distance has changed from what is shown in the *Front View,* change the length of the spindles to compensate.

Trim the spindles to the proper length. Make the tenons on the top and bottom ends on a drill press. Then cut the tapers in the spindles with a hand plane. Still using the plane, round over the corners of the spindles, making them roughly cylindrical toward the top end, as shown in *Section A.*

10 **Attach the back to the rocker.** Dry assemble the back brace, back posts, spindles, and headrest to make sure the parts fit properly. When you're satisfied they do, finish sand all the wood surfaces *except* the front surface of the headrest.

Clamp the back brace to the seat so the back edges are flush. Drill and counterbore three pilot holes for wood screws, up through the seat and into the brace. Secure the brace with flathead wood screws — do *not* glue the brace to the seat.

Glue the bottom ends of the back posts and spindles in the back brace. Before the glue dries, glue the headrest to the top ends. Clamp the headrest in place, making sure it's centered from side to side. Then drill 1/2"-diameter, 1 1/2"-deep holes through the headrest and into the back posts. Cut lengths of 1/2"-diameter dowel and glue them in the holes. When the glue dries, cut the dowels flush with the surface, then sand the front of the headrest.

11 **Cut the arms and arm supports.** Enlarge the *Arm Pattern* and *Arm Support Pattern* and trace them onto the stock. Cut the shapes on a band saw, and make the tenons on a drill press.

Hold each arm support up to the side of the rocker

in the position you want to mount it. Mark the angled notch in the edge of the support. Also mark where the notch will fit over the edge of the seat. Cut the sides of each notch with a dovetail saw or coping saw, then remove the waste with a chisel.

12 **Fit the arms and arm supports to the rocker.** Drill the round mortises for the arm supports in the side rungs, using a hand-held power drill and a spade bit. Put the point of the bit where you've marked the location of each mortise. Sight down

the bit shaft, lining it up with the mortise mark and the mark on the side of the seat where the support will be attached. When the shaft and the marks are aligned, drill the mortise. Back up the side rungs on the bottom face to prevent tear-out.

Temporarily fit the arm supports to the rocker assembly. Hold each arm in place so you can gauge the angle of the round mortise in the back post. Mark the locations of the mortises and remove the arms. Drill the mortises, eyeballing the angles.

Fit the arms to the back posts, and mark the locations of the round mortises for the top ends of the arm supports. Mark the angle of these mortises on the inside edges of the arms. Remove the arms from the posts and drill the mortises.

13 **Attach the arms and arm supports to the rocker.** Temporarily dry assemble the arms with the posts and arm supports. Mark the wedge slots in the top ends of the arm supports — these must be perpendicular to the grain of the arms.

Disassemble the parts and cut the slots with a band saw. Round over the edges of the arms and arm supports with a shaper or router and a ½" quarter-round bit or cutter. Finish sand the wooden surfaces of the parts, *except* the top surfaces of the arms.

Attach the arm supports and arms to the rocker with glue. Cut wedges from scrap stock and tape them into the slots. Also, drill ½"-diameter, 2³⁄₄"-deep holes through the outside edges of the arm supports and into the seat. Cut lengths of ½"-diameter dowel and drive them into the holes so about ¼" of each dowel protrudes from its hole.

When the glue dries, round over the ends of the dowels. Cut the arm support tenons flush with the top surfaces of the arms, then finish sand the arms.

14 **Finish the rocker.** Do any necessary touch-up sanding, then apply a finish. The rocker shown is stained a light brown, then covered with a mixture of one part spar varnish to seven parts tung oil. This creates a hard, durable semi-gloss finish.

You may also elect to paint your rocker. Cottage furniture was often painted a solid color to hide inexpensive woods, then decorated with Victorian designs.

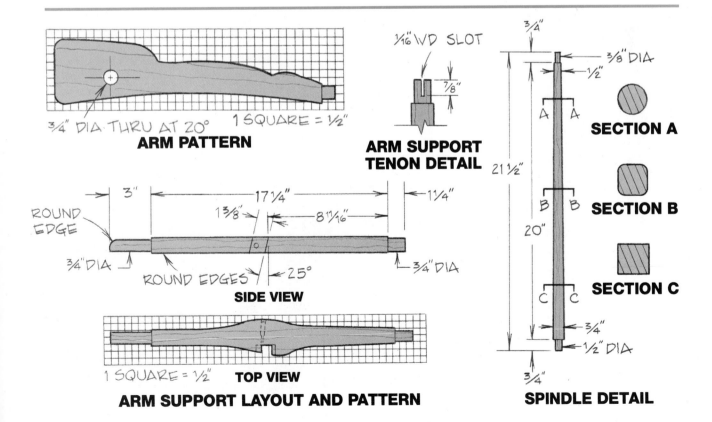

ARM PATTERN

ARM SUPPORT TENON DETAIL

ARM SUPPORT LAYOUT AND PATTERN

SPINDLE DETAIL

Shaker Bench

Shaker craftsmen and craftswomen believed that unnecessary ornamentation was a sin; that true beauty sprang from utility and economy. Consequently, much of their furniture was austere, although graceful and well-proportioned.

This plank bench — a copy of a nineteenth-century antique built by the Shakers of Mount Lebanon, New York — is a good example. The woodworkers reduced its design to the simplest elements. There are just four planks, whereas most similar pieces of that time had five or six. Nonetheless, it's as durable as a five-board bench, and more appealing than many traditional bench designs. With its judicious use of simple, symmetrical arcs to form the feet and reduce the mass, the piece appears light and balanced.

Materials List

FINISHED DIMENSIONS

PART

A.	Seat	$^3/_4$″ x 12″ x 24″
B.	Legs (2)	$^3/_4$″ x 12″ x 15$^5/_8$″
C.	Brace	$^3/_4$″ x 11$^1/_4$″ x 18$^1/_2$″

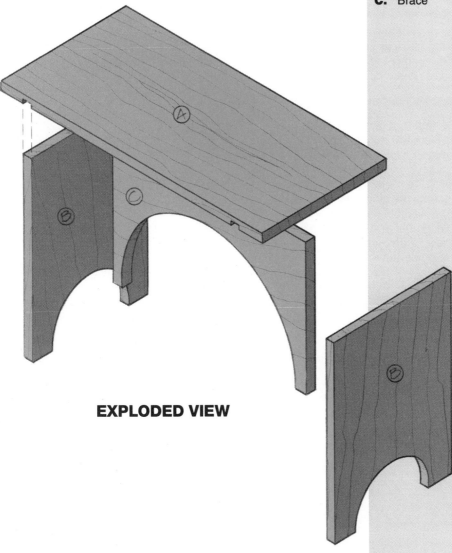

EXPLODED VIEW

HARDWARE

#10 x 1$^1/_4$″ Flathead wood screws
(12–16)

1 Select the stock and cut the parts to size.

To make this project, you need about 7 board feet of 4/4 (four-quarters) stock. You can use almost any hardwood or softwood, but old-time utilitarian pieces such as these were usually built from pine, poplar, or maple. The bench shown is made of poplar.

When you have selected the stock, plane it to ³/₄″ thick. Cut the parts to the sizes given in the Materials List.

2 Cut the dadoes.

The legs fit in two ³/₄″-wide, ³/₈″-deep dadoes in the underside of the top. Cut these dadoes with a dado cutter or a router. If you use a router, cut each dado in several passes, going just ¹/₈″ deeper with each pass.

TRY THIS! To help rout dadoes in wide stock, make a simple T-square from two scraps of plywood — a long arm and a shorter cross. Mount a straight bit in the router and cut a dado in the cross of the "T," keeping the router base against the arm. Lay this jig across the stock, lining up the dado in the cross with the layout lines on the stock. Also use the cross to align the arm perpendicular to the edge. Clamp the jig to the stock and rout the dado, using the arm to guide the router.

3"
³/₄"
27"
3"
³/₄"
³/₄" WD x ¹/₂" DP DADO
12-³/₄"

**T-SQUARE JIG
EXPLODED VIEW**

3

Cut the shapes of the legs and brace. Stack the legs face to face, and tape the stack together with double-faced carpet tape. (You may also nail them together with wire brads.) Make sure the ends and edges are flush.

Lay out an arc on the top leg in the stack, as shown in the *Side View*. Also draw an arc on the brace, as shown in the *Front View*. Cut these arcs with a band saw or saber saw, and sand the sawed edges. Take the leg stack apart and discard the tape (or brads).

4

Assemble the bench. Finish sand the parts, being careful not to round over adjoining ends or edges. Glue the parts together, then reinforce the glue joints with flathead wood screws. Counterbore

and countersink the screws, and cover the heads with wooden plugs. Sand the plugs flush with the wood surface. This will make the bench look as if it's pegged together.

5

Finish the bench. Do any necessary touch-up sanding on the bench, then apply a finish to all surfaces. Benches like these were usually painted — the antique that was the model for this bench was

painted with blue milk paint. The copy is painted with flat latex, then covered with a top coat of boiled linseed oil to simulate an old-time milk paint finish.

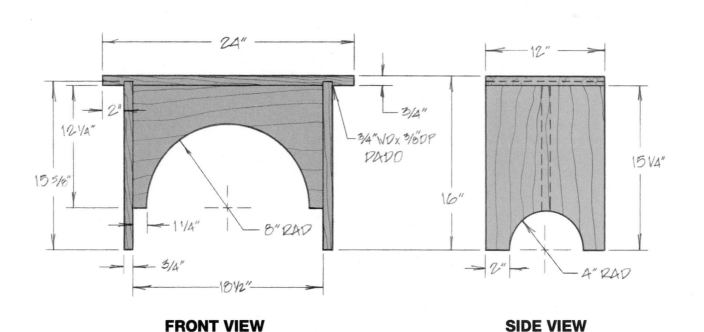

FRONT VIEW   **SIDE VIEW**

Variations

Although the Shaker Bench is a copy of a historical design, it has a very contemporary look. Furthermore, you can make a contemporary, informal dining set by building several benches, then enlarging the bench design to make the table.

Build the table in almost exactly the same manner that you built the bench. However, make the parts from ³⁄₄″ cabinet-grade plywood. Cover the straight edges of the tabletop and legs with 1 x 1 strips to hide the plies. Fasten these strips to the plywood with splines, as shown in the *Edging Detail*. Cover the curved edges of the legs and the braces with veneer banding. (See Figure 1.)

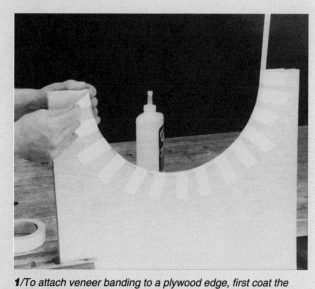

1/*To attach veneer banding to a plywood edge, first coat the edge with glue. Then fasten banding in place with strips of masking tape. This tape stretches slightly, and will keep the glue under pressure while it dries. When the glue is dry, remove and discard the tape.*

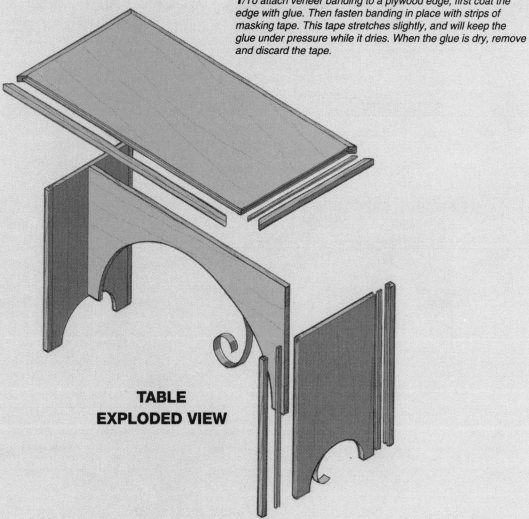

**TABLE
EXPLODED VIEW**

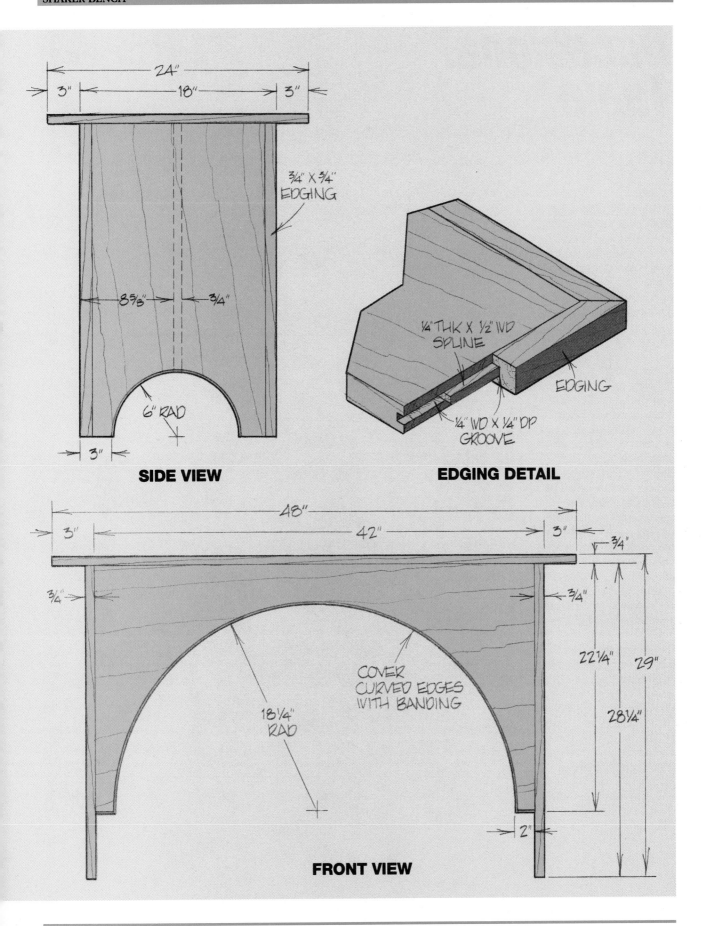

SIDE VIEW

24"

3" 18" 3"

¾" X ¾" EDGING

8⅝" ¾"

6" RAD

3"

EDGING DETAIL

¼" THK X ½" WD SPLINE

EDGING

¼" WD X ¼" DP GROOVE

FRONT VIEW

48"

3" 42" 3"

¾"

¾" ¾"

22¼" 29"

18¼" RAD

COVER CURVED EDGES WITH BANDING

28¼"

2"

Occasional Table

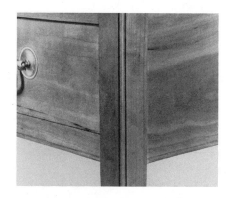

Small "occasional" tables first appeared in the seventeenth century. As the name suggests, they were used on occasion when folks needed additional table space for cooking, serving, dining, or working. And they're still useful, not just for the aforementioned activities, but for dozens of other purposes as well.

This particular occasional table was inspired by an early nineteenth-century antique. The slender, tapered legs echo the popular Hepplewhite style of that era. The single, shallow drawer is typical, too — craftsmen often added a drawer to enhance the utility of the table.

John Parsons, Director of the Wood Technology and Craftsmanship Program at the University of Cincinnati, designed this table as a project for his beginning students. "It's a simple piece," explains John, "but it incorporates many basic joints — rabbet, dado, groove, mortise and tenon, and dovetail. It's a good exercise in joinery, and the students end up with something useful and beautiful."

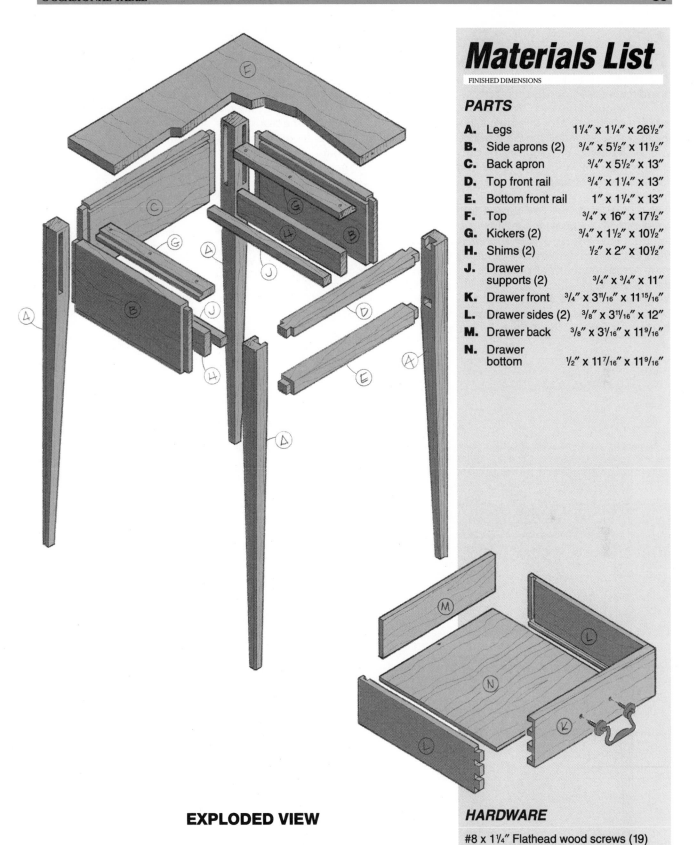

EXPLODED VIEW

Materials List

FINISHED DIMENSIONS

PARTS

A. Legs — $1\frac{1}{4}'' \times 1\frac{1}{4}'' \times 26\frac{1}{2}''$

B. Side aprons (2) — $\frac{3}{4}'' \times 5\frac{1}{2}'' \times 11\frac{1}{2}''$

C. Back apron — $\frac{3}{4}'' \times 5\frac{1}{2}'' \times 13''$

D. Top front rail — $\frac{3}{4}'' \times 1\frac{1}{4}'' \times 13''$

E. Bottom front rail — $1'' \times 1\frac{1}{4}'' \times 13''$

F. Top — $\frac{3}{4}'' \times 16'' \times 17\frac{1}{2}''$

G. Kickers (2) — $\frac{3}{4}'' \times 1\frac{1}{2}'' \times 10\frac{1}{2}''$

H. Shims (2) — $\frac{1}{2}'' \times 2'' \times 10\frac{1}{2}''$

J. Drawer supports (2) — $\frac{3}{4}'' \times \frac{3}{4}'' \times 11''$

K. Drawer front — $\frac{3}{4}'' \times 3\frac{11}{16}'' \times 11\frac{15}{16}''$

L. Drawer sides (2) — $\frac{3}{8}'' \times 3\frac{11}{16}'' \times 12''$

M. Drawer back — $\frac{3}{8}'' \times 3\frac{1}{16}'' \times 11\frac{9}{16}''$

N. Drawer bottom — $\frac{1}{2}'' \times 11\frac{7}{16}'' \times 11\frac{9}{16}''$

HARDWARE

#8 x 1¼″ Flathead wood screws (19)
Drawer pull

1

***Select the stock and cut the parts to
size.*** To make this project, you need about 7
board feet of 4/4 (four-quarters) stock, and 4 board feet
of 6/4 (six-quarters) stock. You can use almost any
cabinet-grade wood for this project; however, because
the legs are so slender, the table will be more durable if
you use hardwoods. Traditionally, early nineteenth-
century tables like these were built from mahogany,
walnut, cherry, or maple. The table shown is built
from cherry.

Plane the 4/4 stock to ³/₄″ thick. Glue up the stock
needed to make the wide top, then cut the top, aprons,
top front rail, kickers, drawer supports, and drawer
front to the sizes shown in the Materials List. Make an
extra apron and drawer front to use as test pieces. Plane
the remaining ³/₄″-thick stock to ¹/₂″, and glue up the
stock needed for the drawer bottom. Cut the drawer
bottom and shims. Then plane the remaining ¹/₂″-thick
stock to ³/₈″ and cut the drawer sides and back.

Cut five rough leg blanks, about 29″ long, from the
6/4 stock. (You'll use the fifth leg as a test piece.) Joint
two adjacent faces of each blank so they are precisely
90° from one another, then plane the remaining two
faces so the blank is 1¹/₄″ square. Cut the legs to length.
Plane the remaining 6/4 stock to 1″ thick and cut two
bottom front rails — one for a test piece and one for
good.

TRY THIS! **Make the drawer parts ¹/₁₆″
wider and longer than specified. This will make
the assembled drawer slightly oversize. You can
plane or file the edges and ends until it fits
perfectly.**

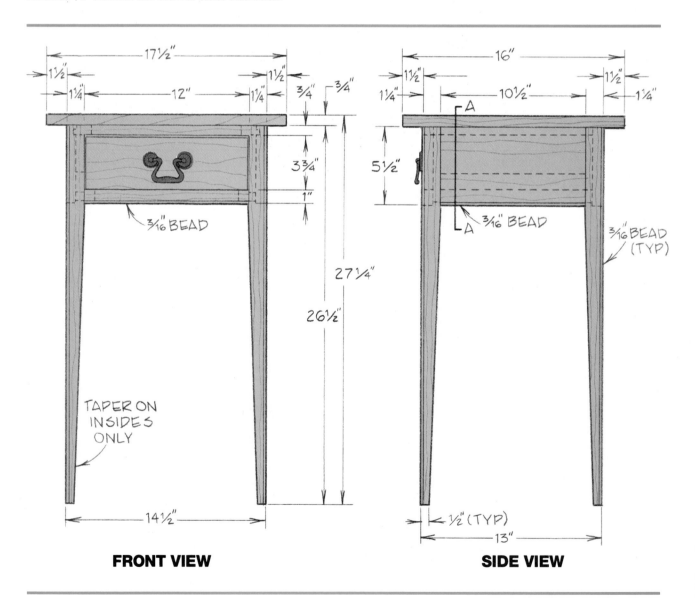

FRONT VIEW   **SIDE VIEW**

2

Cut the mortises and tenons. The legs are joined to the aprons with mortises and tenons. Cut the mortises first, then fit the tenons to them.

Lay out the mortises as shown in the *Right Front Leg Layout* and *Back Leg Layout*. Note that the right and left front legs are mirror images of each other. To make the mortises for the aprons and bottom front rail, drill a line

of overlapping holes, then clean up the sides and square the corners with a chisel. To make the dovetail mortises for the top front rail, first bore out most of the waste with a ⅝″-diameter drill bit. (See Figure 1.) Then remove the remaining waste with a chisel. (See Figure 2.) When setting up to cut each joint, practice first on the test leg, then cut the good stock.

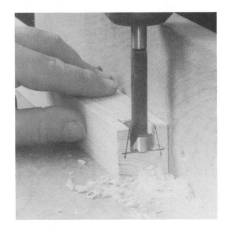

1/To rough out the dovetail mortises in the legs, bore holes near the top ends. Use a Forstner bit if you have one — it leaves a flat bottom.

2/After roughing out the dovetail mortise on the drill press, carefully pare away the remaining waste in the mortise with a chisel.

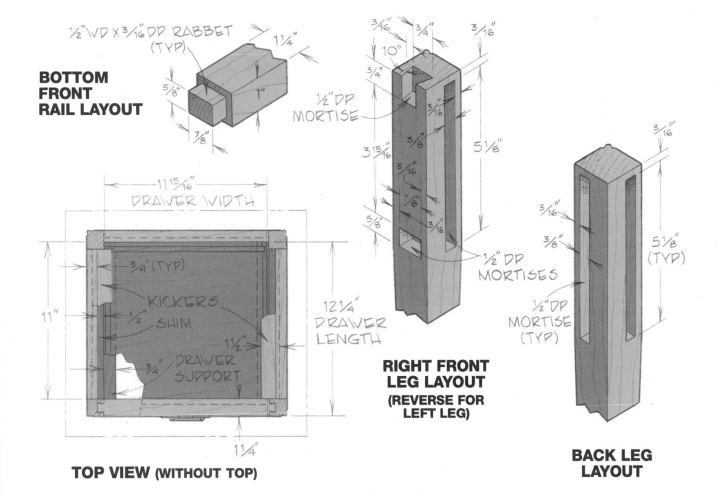

BOTTOM FRONT RAIL LAYOUT

½″ WD X 3/16″ DP RABBET (TYP)

1¼″

⅝″

1″

⅞″

TOP VIEW (WITHOUT TOP)

11 15/16″ DRAWER WIDTH

¾″ (TYP)

KICKERS

SHIM

½″

1½″

¾″ DRAWER SUPPORT

11″

12¼″ DRAWER LENGTH

1¼″

RIGHT FRONT LEG LAYOUT (REVERSE FOR LEFT LEG)

3/16″ ¾″ 3/16″

10°

¾″

3/16″

3 15/16″

3/8″

3/16″

7/8″

5/8″

3/16″

½″ DP MORTISE

3/16″

5⅛″

½″ DP MORTISES

BACK LEG LAYOUT

3/16″

3/16″

3/8″

½″ DP MORTISE (TYP)

5⅛″ (TYP)

Using a dado cutter or a table-mounted router, cut a ³⁄₈"-thick tenon in the end of the practice apron, as shown in the *Apron Layout*. (See Figure 3.) Test fit the tenon in one of the ³⁄₈"-wide mortises. If the tenon is too loose, lower the bit or cutter slightly and make another tenon; if too tight, raise the bit or cutter. When the tenon fits properly, cut all the tenons in the ends of the aprons. Repeat this procedure for the bottom front rail.

To make the dovetail tenons in the ends of the top front rail, lay out the dovetail shape on both ends of the board. Using a band saw or dovetail saw, cut the tenon shapes, sawing a little wide of the layout lines. Test fit the tenons to the dovetail mortises in the legs. Since you cut them wide, they should be tight. Carefully shave or file the tenons until they fit properly.

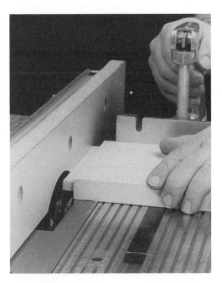
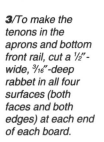

3/To make the tenons in the aprons and bottom front rail, cut a ¹⁄₂"-wide, ⁹⁄₁₆"-deep rabbet in all four surfaces (both faces and both edges) at each end of each board.

TRY THIS! You can also cut the rectangular mortises with a plunge router, if you wish. Clamp three legs side by side in a vise so the faces are flush — this will provide a wide surface to support the router. Rout the mortise in the *middle* leg, keeping the router guide against one of the outer legs. Switch the positions of the legs to cut all the mortises.

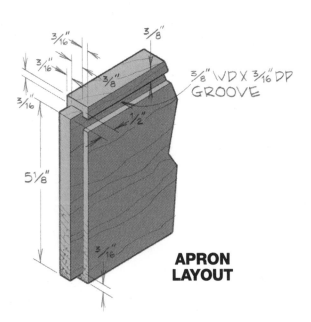

3⁄16"
3⁄8"
3⁄16"
3⁄8"
3⁄16"
³⁄₈" WD X ³⁄₁₆" DP GROOVE
1⁄2"
5¹⁄₈"
³⁄₁₆"

APRON LAYOUT

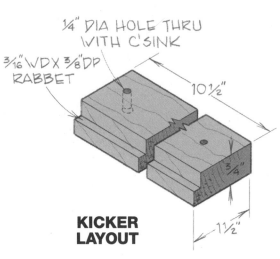

¼" DIA HOLE THRU WITH C'SINK
³⁄₁₆" WD X ³⁄₈" DP RABBET
10½"
¾"
1½"

KICKER LAYOUT

3 **Cut the rabbets and grooves.** While the table saw or router is set up to make joints, cut the interlocking rabbets and grooves in the aprons and kickers. These joints will hold the top to the table.

First, cut ³/₈″-wide, ³/₁₆″-deep grooves in the inside faces of the side aprons, near the top edges, as shown in the *Apron Layout*. Then cut ³/₁₆″-wide, ³/₈″-deep rabbets in the outside edges of the kickers, as shown in the *Kicker Layout,* putting a step in the edges to fit the apron grooves.

Note: The purpose of the kickers is threefold. First, they secure the top to the table assembly. Second, they help prevent the top from cupping or warping. And third, they keep the drawer from tilting forward when you slide it out of the table.

4 **Cut the decorative beads.** The outside corners of the legs and the bottom edges of the side aprons, back apron, and bottom front apron all have a decorative bead, as shown in the *Front View* and *Side View*. You can cut these beads with a machine, using a router, shaper, or molder; or by hand, using a scratch stock. (See Figures 4, 5, and 6.)

5/To make the beads in the corners of the legs, make two cuts in each leg — one in each outside surface. These cuts should overlap to form a single bead at the corner.

4/Cut single ³/₁₆″ beads in the bottom edge of each apron. If you're using a bit or cutter that makes multiple beads, move the fence or adjust the height of the cutter to cover all but one bead.

6/You can cut the beads by hand with a **scratch stock** if you have one. This tool looks like a spokeshave and works like a scraper. It scrapes away the wood, leaving a decorative shape in the surface.

5 **Cut the tapers in the legs.** The legs taper from 1¼″ at the top to ½″ at the bottom, as shown in the *Leg Layout*. Note that the tapers begin 5½″ *below* the top ends of the legs, and only the *inside* faces of each leg are tapered.

To cut the tapers, first make a tapering jig from a scrap of plywood, as shown in the *Tapering Jig Layout*. Use this jig to guide the leg stock as you cut the tapers on a band saw or table saw. (See Figure 7.)

*7/To make the tapers, place the leg stock in the jig with the bottom end fitted in the notch. Feed the jig and the leg into the blade, cutting the first taper. Turn the leg 90° so the first taper faces **up** and cut the second taper.* **Saw guard removed for clarity.**

6 **Drill the pilot holes in the kickers.** The kickers are attached to the top with six screws, three in each kicker. The pilot holes for these screws must be slightly oversize to allow for the expansion and contraction of the top — as the top moves, the screws will shift in the holes.

Drill three ¼″-diameter pilot holes through the face of each kicker, as shown in the *Kicker Layout*. The positions of these holes are not critical, but they should be evenly spaced along the length of each kicker. Cut a countersink in each hole, so the screw heads will be flush with the bottom surface of the kickers.

7 **Assemble the table.** Finish sand the legs, aprons, top, and rails. Be careful not to round over adjoining ends or edges. Lightly sand the surfaces of the kickers, shims, and drawer supports where the drawer will rub — this will help the drawer to slide smoothly.

Dry assemble the legs, aprons, and rails *without* glue to test the fit of the mortise-and-tenon joints. When you're satisfied they fit properly, reassemble them with glue. Carefully check that the aprons and rails are square, the legs are plumb, and the top surfaces of the legs and aprons are flush as you clamp the parts together.

Let the glue dry overnight and remove the clamps. Glue the shims to the side aprons, then reinforce each shim with three screws. Countersink the heads of the screws so the heads are flush with (or slightly below) the wood surface, as shown in *Section A*.

Clamp the drawer supports to the shims. Check the position of the drawer supports carefully — they must be flush with the top surface of the bottom front rail, and perfectly parallel with the top edge of the side aprons. When you're sure the supports are properly positioned, drill three screw holes through each support and into the shims. Remove the clamps, then

secure the supports to the shims with glue and screws.

Turn the top upside down on your workbench, then turn the table assembly upside down on the top. Position the assembly so it is inset from the top by 1½″ on all sides, and clamp the assembly to the top. Put the kickers in place, inserting the rabbeted edges in the side apron grooves. Drill pilot holes in the top, using the holes in the kickers as guides. *Be careful not to drill completely through the top!* Secure the kickers to the top with screws. Do *not* glue the kickers to the top or aprons.

TRY THIS! Wipe away any glue that squeezes out of the joints with a *wet* (not just damp) rag. The rag must be wet enough to dissolve any glue in the pores of the wood and wash it away completely. This will raise the grain slightly, but you'll find it's less work to sand the raised grain than it is to scrape away glue beads.

8

Cut the drawer dovetails. The drawer sides are fastened to the front with half-blind dovetails — these dovetails can't be seen from the front of the drawer. Cut the tails in the sides first, then the pins in the front.

Lay out the tails on the front ends of the drawer sides as shown in the *Dovetail Layout*. Carefully cut the sides or "cheeks" of the tails with a dovetail saw, cutting to the inside of the layout lines. Remove the waste with a chisel. (See Figures 8, 9, and 10.)

8/Cut the cheeks of the tails with a dovetail saw. If you wish, use a small wooden square to help keep the saw perpendicular to the stock. You can make this square from hardwood scraps.

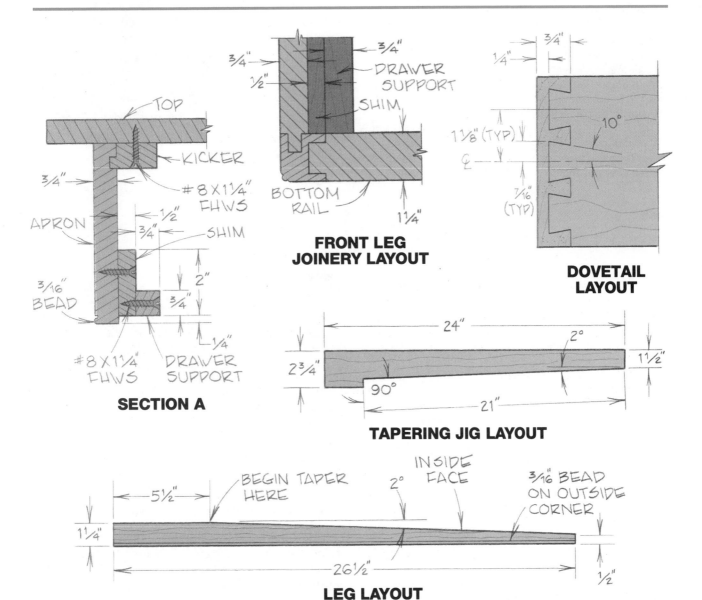

FRONT LEG JOINERY LAYOUT

DOVETAIL LAYOUT

SECTION A

TAPERING JIG LAYOUT

LEG LAYOUT

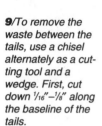

9/To remove the waste between the tails, use a chisel alternately as a cutting tool and a wedge. First, cut down ¹/₁₆″–¹/₈″ along the baseline of the tails.

10/Then drive the chisel into the end grain, wedging out a sliver of waste. Repeat until you've cut halfway through the waste. Turn the drawer side over and finish removing the waste from the other side.

Use the completed tails as a template to lay out the pins on the ends of the drawer front. Cut these pins using the same method you used to cut the dovetail mortises in the ends of the legs. Rough out the pins on the drill press, removing as much waste as you can by drilling 1″-diameter blind holes. Then cut away the remaining waste with a chisel, cutting slightly *inside* the layout lines. (See Figure 11.) Once again, you'll find it helpful to cut one or two practice pins in the test drawer front, then cut the good stock.

Test fit the pins and tails. Because you've consistently cut to the insides of the layout lines, the fit should be tight. If it's too tight, remove some stock from the tails with a chisel or file until they fit the pins properly.

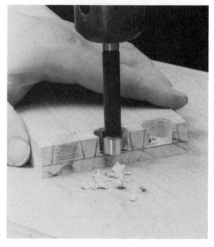

11/Remove as much waste as you can from between the pins with a 1″-diameter drill bit. Later, you can cut away the remaining waste with a chisel.

9 **Cut the drawer dadoes and grooves.**
The remaining parts of the drawer are assembled with dadoes and grooves, as shown in the *Drawer/Top View*. Using a dado cutter or a table-mounted router, cut ³/₈″-wide, ³/₁₆″-deep dadoes near the back ends of the drawer sides to hold the drawer back. Then cut ³/₈″-wide, ³/₁₆″-deep grooves near the bottom edges of the drawer sides and drawer front to hold the drawer bottom.

TRY THIS! If you wish, cut a *double-blind* groove in the drawer front, stopping ³/₁₆″ from each end. (It's easiest to cut blind joints with a router — you can see where to stop cutting.) Square the blind ends of the grooves with a chisel. This way, you won't see the ends of the grooves when you assemble the drawer, and the completed drawer will look neater.

10 **Assemble and fit the drawer.** Dry assemble the drawer front, back, and sides to test the fit of the parts. Using a hand plane, chamfer the edges and ends of the drawer bottom on the underside, so the bottom fits the grooves. Slide the bottom in place.

When you're satisfied that all the drawer parts fit properly, disassemble the drawer. Finish sand the drawer front and lightly sand the other parts. Reassemble the drawer front, back, and sides with glue. Slide the bottom in place and secure it to the back with a single screw, as shown in the *Drawer/Back View*. Do *not* glue the drawer bottom in place. Let it "float" in the grooves so it can expand and contract.

Install a drawer pull on the drawer front, then test fit the drawer in the table. If you've made the drawer parts slightly oversize, the drawer shouldn't fit — yet. Plane and sand the top edges and side surfaces until the drawer slides smoothly in and out of the opening. Sand the back ends of the drawer sides so they butt against the back apron when the drawer front is flush with the rails.

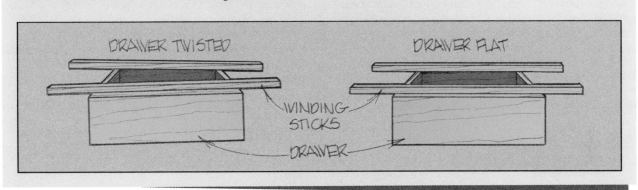

TRY THIS! When clamping the drawer parts together, lay two "winding sticks" across the top edges of the front and back. These sticks should be ½″ square, about 24″ long, and made from two different colors of wood. Sight across the sticks, front to back, to make sure they're parallel. If they aren't, loosen or tighten the clamps until they are. This will ensure that the drawer assembly is flat when the glue dries.

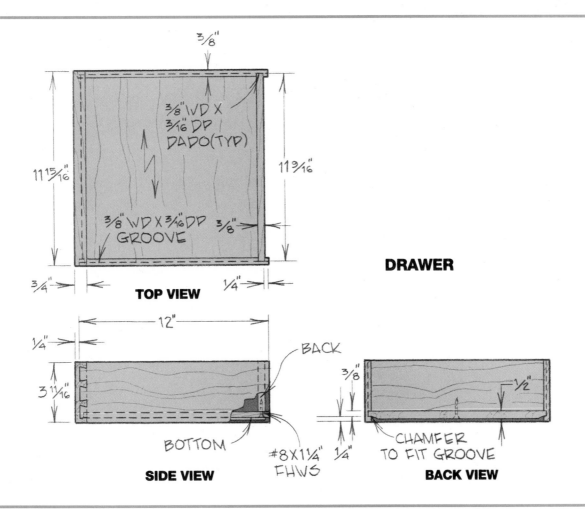

DRAWER

TRY THIS! If you're building this project in the summer, fit the drawer to the opening with as little slop as possible. The drawer will shrink in the winter and become looser. If you're building it in the winter, fit the drawer with 1/16"–1/8" of slop. This will give the drawer room to expand so it won't stick in the summer. If it's spring or fall, split the difference — fit the drawer with 1/32"–1/16" of slop.

11 Finish the table. Remove the drawer from the opening, and the pull from the drawer. Place the table on a flat surface and check that it doesn't wobble. If it does, mark the high leg and remove stock from the bottom end with a file or sander until the table is stable.

Do any necessary touch-up sanding, then apply a finish to all wooden surfaces. Be sure to apply as many coats to the underside of the tabletop and the insides of the aprons as you do to the surfaces that show. This will help keep the table from warping or twisting.

Rub out the finish and apply a coat of paste wax to all wood surfaces that show. Rub paraffin wax on the drawer supports and shims — this will help the drawer to slide smoothly. Replace the pull on the drawer and insert the drawer in its opening.

Variations

During the eighteenth and nineteenth centuries, craftsmen often added drop leaves to occasional tables to increase the available surface area. These small drop-leaf tables were called *breakfast tables* or *Pembroke tables*.

To add drop leaves to this particular table, eliminate the kickers at the sides. Cut out the side aprons to make drop leaf supports, as shown in the *Drop Leaf Support Layout,* and install them with roundhead wood screws as pivots.

Make each drop leaf 3/4" thick, 8 3/4" wide, and 16" long. Mount these to the top with drop-leaf hinges. Mount a single kicker beneath the top, toward the middle of the table. Then attach the top assembly to the top front rail and back apron.

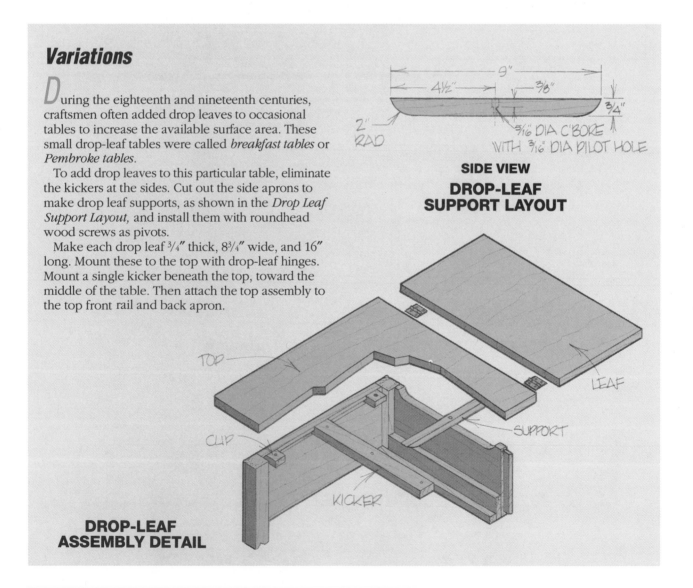

SIDE VIEW
DROP-LEAF SUPPORT LAYOUT

DROP-LEAF ASSEMBLY DETAIL

Three-Legged Stool

A stool is an uncomplicated construction. In its basic form, it's nothing more than a plank supported by three or four legs. But despite this simplicity, it doesn't have to be unsophisticated. The three-legged high stool featured here is as well-crafted and appealing as many of the best chairs.

It was built by Randall Fields of Amesville, Ohio. Randy considers himself a "progressive" Windsor chairmaker — he makes contemporary seating derived from traditional Windsor forms. The design for this stool was inspired by the ancient three-legged plank stool that was the humble beginning of Windsor seats. This rustic English form evolved into highly crafted chairs and settees as turners elaborated on the stool, adding legs, rungs, and back pieces.

To make this stool, Randall reversed this evolution, cutting the Windsor chair back to its most basic form. However, he kept some of the refinements, such as the saddle seat and the tapered legs and rungs. ✳

Materials List

FINISHED DIMENSIONS

PARTS

A. Seat $1^3/4''$ x $13^1/4''$ x $13^9/{16}''$
B. Legs (3) $1^1/2''$ dia. x 27″
C. Top rung $1^1/4''$ dia. x 13″
D. Middle rung $1^1/4''$ dia. x $13^1/2''$
E. Bottom rung $1^1/4''$ dia. x 14″
F. Leg wedges $3/{32}''$ x $7/8''$ x $1^1/2''$
G. Rung wedges $3/{32}''$ x $5/8''$ x $1^1/4''$

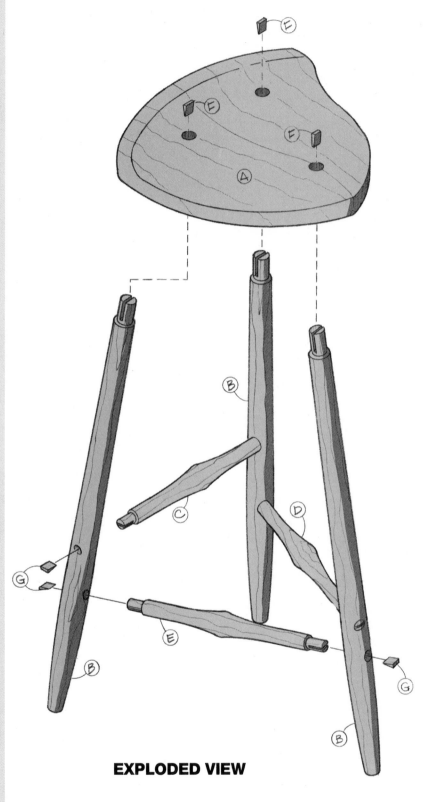

EXPLODED VIEW

1

Select the stock and cut the parts to rough size. To make this project, you need about 8 board feet of 8/4 (eight-quarters) stock. You can use almost any cabinet-grade wood, although hardwoods will wear better. Historically, the turned parts of American Windsor furniture were made from maple, chestnut, hickory, or oak, and the seats were made from poplar or white pine. On the stool shown, the turned parts are maple and the seat and wedges are walnut.

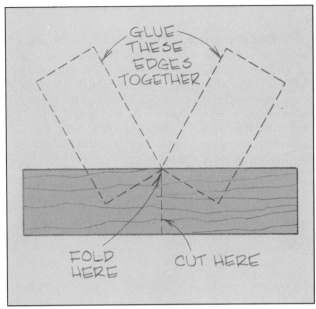

TRY THIS! Randall uses contrasting colors of wood for the turned parts and the wedges. This creates a decorative effect and emphasizes the well-planned, well-crafted joinery.

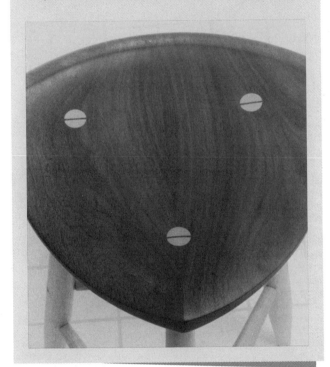

1/Select a board at least 7″ wide and 28″ long to make the seat. Cut the board in half and fold one edge against itself. Glue the parts together.

When you cut the shape of the seat, make sure the grain runs back to front, and the seam is in the middle of the seat.

TRY THIS! Although many turners round their spindles directly from square boards, Randall finds he can save time and chisels if he knocks off the corners on a table saw, making each turning square into an octagon.

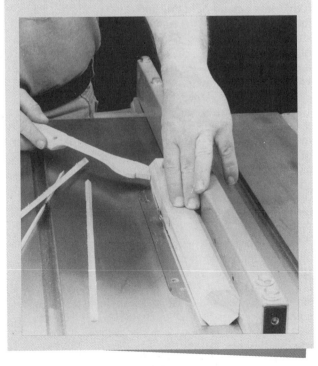

Plane the rough-cut wood, removing just enough stock to see the grain. Decide which portions of the wood you will use for each part. Then plane the seat stock to 1³/₄″ thick. Since it's difficult to find 14″-wide 8/4 stock, you'll probably have to glue up wood to make the wide board for the seat. Randall has found that he can create a pleasing grain pattern if he glues up two parts for the seat from the same 7″-wide board. He cuts the board in half, then folds one edge against itself, as shown in Figure 1.

Set aside a little piece of stock to make the wedges, then cut the remaining wood into turning squares for the legs and rungs. Each turning square should be 1″–2″ longer than specified in the Materials List — this will give you some extra stock at each end.

2

Cut the shape of the seat. Decide which surface of the seat stock will be the bottom, then lay out the round leg mortises and the seat shape on it. Mark the leg mortises first. Determine the center of the seat — remember, the center should be on the seam — and scribe a circle with a radius of 4¼″ inches. Then draw three lines radiating from the center out to the circle. One line should be on the seam, and the other two 120° to the right and left of it, as shown in the *Leg Mortise Layout*. Mark the positions of the leg mortises where the lines intersect the circle.

From each leg mortise mark, scribe an arc with a 10⅛″ radius past the other two marks. The arcs will intersect, forming a triangle that bulges at the sides, as shown in the *Seat Layout*. This is the shape of the seat. Cut the shape with a band saw or fretsaw, and sand the sawed edges.

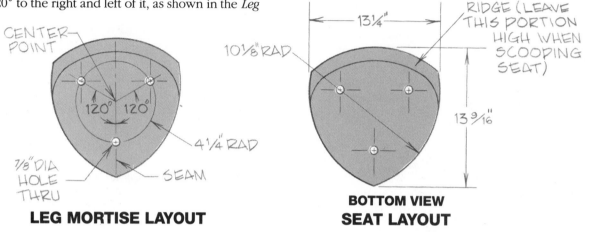

LEG MORTISE LAYOUT

**BOTTOM VIEW
SEAT LAYOUT**

3

Drill the leg mortises in the seat. The leg mortises are round holes, ⅞″ in diameter. These holes are angled so the legs splay out from the seat at 12° off perpendicular, as shown in the *Side View*.

Bore the round mortises through the seat from the bottom, using a hand-held drill and a ⅞″ spade bit. To judge the angle, make a simple mortising guide, as shown in the *Mortising Guide* drawing. Cut a 6″ length of coat hanger wire. Drill a hole the same diameter as the wire through the center of a ¾″ x 2″ x 2″ scrap of wood. Glue the wire in the wood with epoxy.

When the epoxy dries, bend the wire so it leans at 12°. Use a protractor and a sliding T-bevel to help set the angle. (See Figure 2.) Place the guide near a mortise mark and orient it so the wire leans out from the center of the seat. Place the point of the spade bit on the mark and sight down the shaft. Try to hold the drill so the bit shaft is parallel with the mortising guide wire. When you're confident the drill is at the correct angle, bore the mortise hole all the way through the seat. (See Figure 3.)

Note: This is not a precision operation — traditionally, craftsmen eyeball the angles of round mortises in Windsor furniture. It won't ruin the project if the angle is a few degrees off. In fact, the completed stool may be stronger because of it. Also, it doesn't matter if there's some tear-out on the top surface where the bit exits the seat. Later, you'll "scoop" a saddle in the seat and remove the torn stock.

2/To determine the angle of the mortising guide, first set a sliding T-bevel to the proper angle with a protractor. Rest the bevel on the workbench, in front of the mortising guide. Sight along the T-bevel and bend the guide wire until it's parallel with the bevel's edge.

3/Place the guide on the seat bottom and turn it until the wire leans in the same direction that you want to drill the round mortise. Hold the drill so the bit shaft looks parallel to the guide wire, and bore through the seat. Don't worry if the drill isn't perfectly parallel to the guide wire — the angle of the mortise doesn't have to be exact.

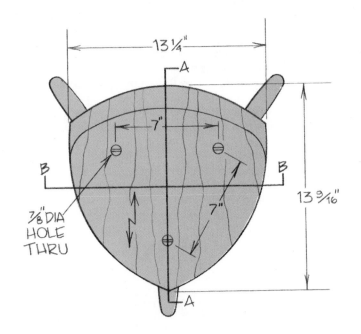

TOP VIEW

13¼"

7"

7"

13 9/16"

3/8" DIA HOLE THRU

A

A

B

B

MORTISING GUIDE

COAT HANGER WIRE

6"

3/4"

2"

2"

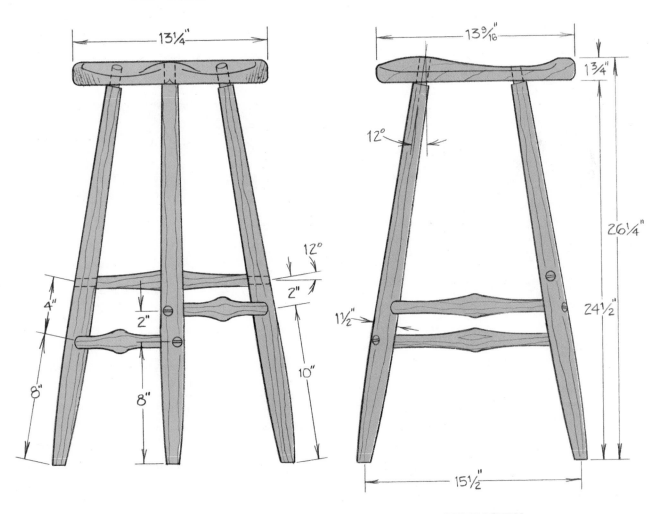

FRONT VIEW

13¼"

12°

2"

4"

2"

8"

8"

10"

SIDE VIEW

13 9/16"

1¾"

12°

26¼"

24½"

1½"

15½"

4 **_Carve the saddle in the seat._** Like most Windsor furniture, this stool has a "saddle" seat, carved to fit a person's backside. There are several ways to carve this saddle — you can use traditional hand tools, such as an inshave and scorp, a router with a ball mill, or even a hand-held circular saw. Refer to Scooping a Chair Seat for specific instructions on various techniques.

When you've chosen a tool and a technique, clamp the seat to your workbench right side up and carve the saddle. Scoop it deeper toward the back than toward the front, as shown in _Section A_. Toward the front,

leave the seat a little higher in the center than at the sides, as shown in _Section B_. This will create the "pommel" of the saddle shape. Round over the seat at the front and the sides and leave a ridge in back.

Note: As with drilling the mortises, you need not be precise when scooping a seat. If your saddle shape is different from the one shown, it will simply make the stool an individual, one-of-a-kind piece.

Turn the seat upside down again. Using a router and a ³⁄₄″ quarter-round bit, round over the _bottom_ edges of the seat, all around the perimeter. Finish sand the bottom of the seat, but don't sand the top yet.

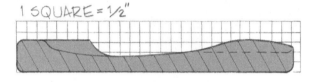

SECTION A

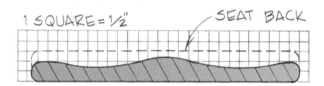

SECTION B

5 **_Turn the legs._** Mount a leg blank on the lathe and turn it to the shape shown in the _Leg Layout_. Be especially careful when you turn the tenon. While other operations in making this stool leave room for imprecision, this doesn't. The tenon must be precisely ⁷⁄₈″ in diameter. To be certain it is, make a jig from a scrap of plywood as shown in the _Tenon Calipers_ drawing. Use this to check the diameter of the work as you turn it. (See Figures 4 and 5.)

After turning the leg shape and the tenon, finish sand the leg on the lathe. Be careful _not_ to sand the tenon. Repeat this process, turning and sanding the remaining two legs. Before removing each leg from the lathe, mark the positions of the rungs. Cut each leg to length on a band saw or table saw, but don't bevel the bottom ends yet.

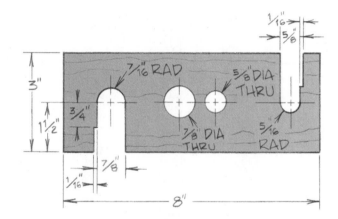

TENON CALIPERS

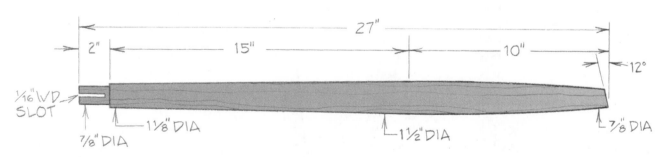

LEG LAYOUT

4/As you turn the tenon, frequently check the diameter by holding the caliper jig against the stock. When the slotted jig slips over the tenon up to the step, the tenon is within 1/16" of the proper diameter.

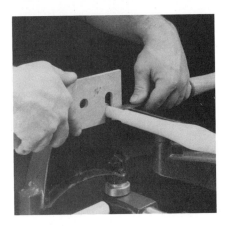

5/Remove the last 1/16" of the tenon with a square-nose chisel. Stop cutting when the caliper jig slips over the tenon, **past** the step — the tenon should be at the proper diameter.

6 Assemble the legs and seat. Temporarily, insert the leg tenons in the round mortises in the seat. Mark a slot for a wedge on the top end of each leg where the tenon pokes through the seat. The wedges must all be perpendicular to the grain direction of the seat. Mark the location of each leg in the seat, so you can later replace the legs in their respective mortises. And mark the bevel on the bottom of the legs. (See Figure 6.)

Remove the legs from the seat and cut the slots for the wedges in the tenons, using a band saw or dovetail saw. Cut the beveled ends of the legs with a dovetail saw. Also, cut wedges from the scrap you set aside. These wedges should be 3/32" at the top end (about 1/32" thicker than the slot is wide), and taper to a point. Replace the legs in the seat and lightly tap the wedges in place. Do *not* glue the legs or the wedges in place yet.

6/To mark the bevel on the legs, Randall uses a pencil taped to a wood scrap. With the scrap resting flat on the workbench, he traces around the circumference of each leg.

7 Drill the rung holes. Drill the round mortises for the rungs through each leg, using a hand-held drill and a 5/8" spade bit. Put the point of the bit on a rung mark and sight along the shaft, pointing the drill at another leg where you've marked the mortise for the other end of the rung. Bore the mortise through the leg, then do the same at the other mark. Repeat, boring all the rung mortises.

TRY THIS! To keep the rung mortise holes from tearing out when the bit exits the wood, stop drilling as soon as the point of the spade bit appears on the opposite side of the leg. Remove the bit from the hole, place the point in the pinhole on the opposite side of the leg, and finish drilling the hole from that side.

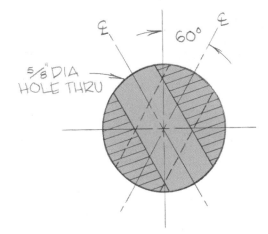

5/8" DIA HOLE THRU

60°

SECTION VIEW

ROUND MORTISE DETAIL

8

Turn the rungs. Measure the distance between each leg at the rung holes, and compare them with the lengths of the rungs specified in the Materials List. If there's a discrepancy of less than ½″, don't worry — the legs will flex that much. If the discrepancy is more than ½″, adjust the length of the rung accordingly.

Turn the rungs as you did the legs, taking care to make the tenons precisely ⅝″ in diameter. Finish sand the rungs on the lathe, then cut them to length.

Remove the legs from the seat and insert the rungs in the rung mortises. Mark the wedge slots on the ends of the rung tenons. Once again, these wedges must be perpendicular to the grain direction of the legs. Mark the position of the rungs in the legs so you can later replace the rungs in their respective mortises. Disassemble the legs and rungs, and cut the slots.

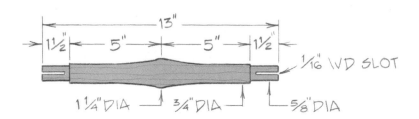

TOP RUNG LAYOUT

9

Assemble the stool. Cut the wedges for the rungs. Make a few extra, in case one breaks or doesn't fit as well as you'd like.

Using a brush, spread a little glue inside the rung mortises. Do *not* spread glue on the tenons. (No matter how or where you apply the glue, some will squeeze out when you assemble the tenons in the mortises. However, it's easier to clean up this excess glue on the outside of the mortise, where the tenon exits the hole, than it is on the inside where the tenon enters.) Insert the rungs in the mortises and rotate them so the slots are properly oriented.

Spread glue inside the leg mortises, and insert the leg tenons in the seat. Make sure that all the legs and rungs are in their correct positions, then wipe a little glue into each slot. Tap the wedges into the slots with a small hammer or mallet.

Let the glue dry, then cut off the protruding tenons and wedges with a coping saw or dovetail saw. Sand the ends of the tenons flush with the surfaces of the legs and seat. At the same time, finish sand the top surface of the seat, removing any tool marks.

10

Finish the stool. Do any necessary touchup sanding, then apply a finish to the stool. Randall prefers to mix up his own wipe-on finish — he blends tung oil, turpentine, and polyurethane in equal proportions, then adds a little japan drier — about ½ teaspoon of drier for each quart of blended finish. The result is a clear, durable finish with a soft sheen. Wipe on several coats with a clean, lint-free cloth, letting it dry several hours between each coat. Rub it out with #0000 steel wool or emery cloth, and buff it with paste wax.

Scooping a Chair Seat

Traditionally, Windsor chairs have "saddle" seats — solid wooden seats, shaped to fit your backside. This shape is carved or scooped from the wood. Old-time Windsor chairmakers once used an adze to scoop seats, but contemporary chairmakers use a variety of tools and techniques.

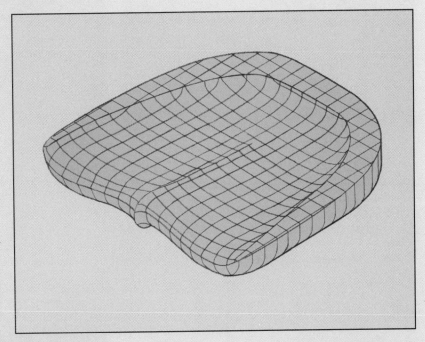

A typical saddle seat is scooped low toward the back and sides, sloping down from the front at 5° to 8°. The chairmaker usually leaves a flat, unshaped ridge at the back, where the back spindles will be attached. He may also carve a gentle crest in the seat, near the front edge, forming the "pommel" of the saddle.

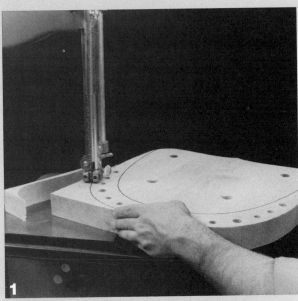

1

Bore the round mortises in the seat **before** shaping it. While the stock is still square, it will be easier to lay out and align the joints accurately. Then cut the shape of the seat on a band saw.

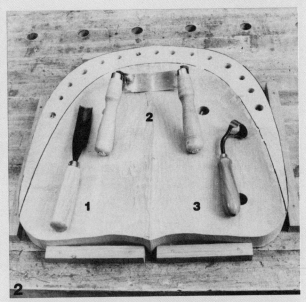

2

You can use several different tools to scoop a seat by hand. In addition to the traditional adze, you may also carve the shape with a bent gouge (1), curved drawknife, or inshave (2), or scorp (3). Novice chairmakers usually find it easiest to rough out the saddle with a gouge, then finish with a scorp. More-experienced craftsmen use an inshave for both the rough and the finish work.

(Continued)

Scooping a Chair Seat — Continued

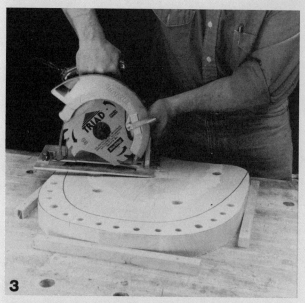

3

If you prefer to work with power tools, try a hand-held circular saw to make a series of cove cuts. Use a triangular curve-cutting blade — this will give you more control. Hold the circular saw reversed (as shown). If the saw kicks back, it will kick out from your body.

4

To begin scooping with a circular saw, adjust the shoe so just ¼" of the blade protrudes. Rest the saw on the front edge or "nose" of the shoe, with the back edge slightly above the stock. Turn on the saw and lower it until you feel it bite. Then move the saw sideways. **Important:** Always cut from left to right — there's more shoe on the right side of the saw to help guide the cut. If you work from right to left, the saw may tip over.

7

For detail work, chair makers traditionally use chisels and gouges. However, you might also try a flexible shaft carving machine. The shaft powers a variety of cutters and accessories that remove large amounts of stock quickly.

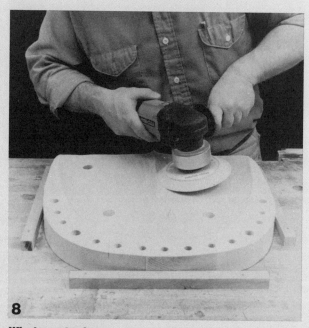

8

Whatever tools you use to shape the seat, use a disk sander or random-orbit sander to grind the final shape. These sanders smooth rough wood quickly, yet leave a very regular surface. The disks on the sanders fit the saddle shape perfectly. Start with a coarse grit — 50# — and work your way to 150#.

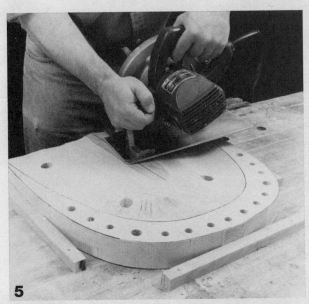

5

With each pass of the saw, *scoop ¹/₃₂"–¹/₁₆" deeper. As the carved portion of the seat gets deeper, readjust the shoe so more and more blade protrudes. Don't try to cut the final seat shape, just rough it out. Later, you can create the final shape with other tools.*

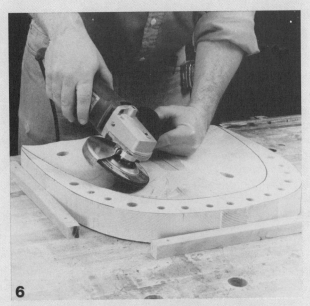

6

You can also use *an angle grinder or sander-grinder to scoop the seat. Use a coarse grinding wheel or very coarse sanding disks (15# or 30#).*

9

After smoothing the scooped portion *of the seat, round over the front and side edges of the seat. When you sit on the finished chair, your body shouldn't contact any hard, square edges.*

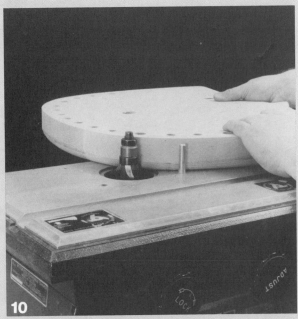

10

Finally, round the bottom edge *of the seat, using a shaper or router and a quarter-round cutter. Sand the bottom surface smooth.*

Sofa Table

The invention of the sofa table is usually credited to the English draftsman and teacher, Thomas Sheraton. In his collection of patterns, *The Cabinet-Maker and Upholsterer's Drawing Book,* published in the 1790s, he included a design for a table "to take a useful place before the sofa." This table was apparently inspired by kitchen sideboards —

long, narrow, waist-high tables for cooking, serving, and (occasionally) eating. However, the sofa table was used to hold lamps, reading materials, game boards, and other items that someone might need while reading or resting.

Sofa tables haven't changed substantially since then. They still have roughly the same simple

function and form as their eighteenth-century ancestors. This contemporary sofa table makes only two small departures from tradition. The first is visible — it has a long

shelf below the tabletop for additional storage. The second is invisible — it uses "knock-down" joinery. The table comes apart easily for moving and storage.

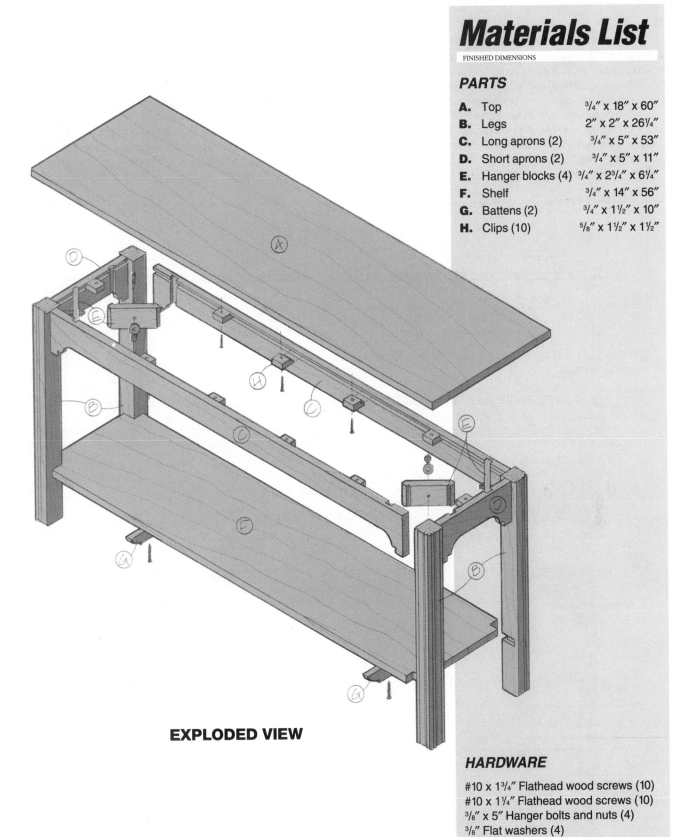

EXPLODED VIEW

Materials List

FINISHED DIMENSIONS

PARTS

A. Top $3/4''$ x 18" x 60"
B. Legs   2" x 2" x $26\frac{1}{4}''$
C. Long aprons (2) $3/4''$ x 5" x 53"
D. Short aprons (2) $3/4''$ x 5" x 11"
E. Hanger blocks (4) $3/4''$ x $2\frac{3}{4}''$ x $6\frac{1}{4}''$
F. Shelf $3/4''$ x 14" x 56"
G. Battens (2) $3/4''$ x $1\frac{1}{2}''$ x 10"
H. Clips (10) $5/8''$ x $1\frac{1}{2}''$ x $1\frac{1}{2}''$

HARDWARE

#10 x $1\frac{3}{4}''$ Flathead wood screws (10)
#10 x $1\frac{1}{4}''$ Flathead wood screws (10)
$3/8''$ x 5" Hanger bolts and nuts (4)
$3/8''$ Flat washers (4)

1

Select the stock and cut the parts to size. To make this project, you need about 21 board feet of 4/4 (four-quarters) stock, and 5 board feet of 10/4 (ten-quarters) stock. You can make a sofa table from almost any cabinet-grade wood, although tables are more durable when made from hardwood. (The harder material resists dents and scratches.) The sofa table shown is made from "wavy" cherry.

After selecting the lumber, plane the 4/4 wood to ³/₄″ thick. Glue up the stock needed to make wide boards for the top and shelf. Cut the top, shelf, aprons, hanger blocks, and battens to the sizes specified in the Materials List. Plane 1 board foot of the remaining 4/4 wood to ⁵/₈″ thick to make the clips, but *don't* cut them to size yet. Set the clip stock aside for now.

Cut five rough leg blanks, about 29″ long, from the 10/4 stock. (You'll use the fifth leg as a test piece.) Joint two adjacent faces on each blank to make them precisely 90° from one another, then plane the remaining two faces so the blank is 2″ square. Cut the legs to length.

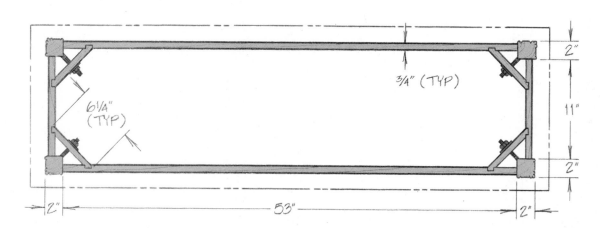

TOP VIEW
(WITHOUT TOP)

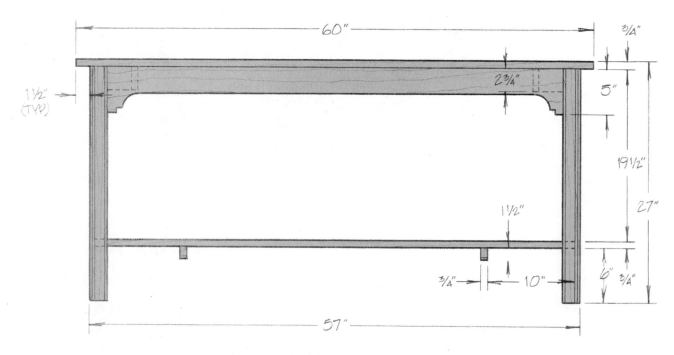

FRONT VIEW

2 **Make the hanger blocks.** The legs are held to the aprons by hanger blocks and bolts, as shown in the *Top View*. These knock-down fixtures allow you to remove the legs from the aprons by loosening four nuts.

To make the hanger blocks, first drill ⁷/₁₆″-diameter holes through the center of the face of each block, as shown in the *Leg Joinery and Hanger Block Detail*. Tilt the blade (or the table) of the table saw to 45°, and mount an extension and a stop block on the miter gauge. This arrangement will automatically position the stock before each cut. Using the miter gauge to guide the stock across the blade, make four bevel cuts across the ends of each block. (See Figure 1.)

First, cut one side of the V-groove near both ends of each block. Make a pass, then flip the block end for end and make another. Readjust the position of the stop block and cut the other side of each groove. (See Figure 2.) After making the grooves, readjust the position of the stop block again and cut a narrow bevel in each end. (See Figure 3.) Move the stop block one last time, and cut a wider bevel. (See Figure 4.) This will complete the shape of the block.

Note: The stop block must be positioned precisely for the last (wide) bevel cut. If the block is too close to the blade, you'll shorten it as you cut the first end. When you flip the block and cut the remaining end, the bevel will be off, making the block asymmetrical.

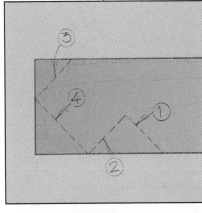

1/To shape the hanger blocks, you'll have to make four bevel cuts in each end of each block. Make the cuts in the sequence shown.

2/To cut the shape of the hanger block, first make two bevel cuts at 45° to form a V-groove near each end. Use a miter gauge extension and a stop block to position the stock before making each cut.

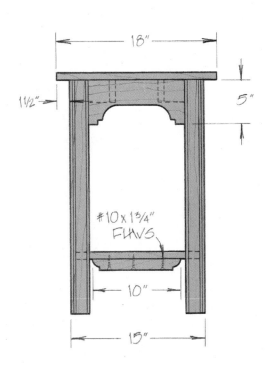

SIDE VIEW

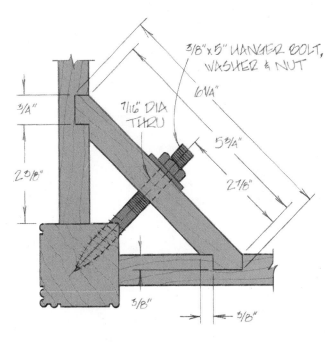

LEG JOINERY AND HANGER BLOCK DETAIL

3/After cutting the V-grooves, cut a narrow bevel in each end of each block. **Saw guard removed for clarity.**

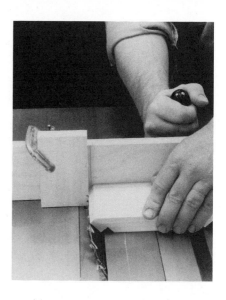

4/Finish the block by cutting a wide bevel in each end. When making this last bevel, position the block very accurately so you don't cut it too short. **Saw guard removed for clarity.**

3 Cut the dadoes and grooves in the legs and aprons.

Most of the parts fit together with simple dadoes and grooves. Make these joints using a dado cutter or a table-mounted router. (See Figures 5, 6, and 7.) Here's a list:

- $3/4''$-wide, $3/8''$-deep dadoes in the aprons to hold the hanger blocks, as shown in the *Leg Joinery and Hanger Block Detail*
- $3/4''$-wide, $3/8''$-deep blind dadoes in the legs to hold the shelf, as shown in the *Front View, Side View,* and *Leg Layout*
- $3/8''$-wide, $3/8''$-deep grooves in the inside faces of the aprons to hold the rabbeted ends of the clips, as shown in the *Tabletop Joinery Detail*

6/The best tool to cut the blind dadoes in the legs is a table-mounted router — it's easier to stop the cut. Clamp a stop block to the table to stop the dado $1/2''$ before the bit exits the outside face of the leg.

5/When cutting the dadoes in the aprons, again use a miter gauge extension and a stop block. However, this time clamp the stop block to the rip fence to help position the stock for each cut. Use the extension on the face of the miter gauge to keep the long boards square to the bit or cutter.

7/After routing the dadoes, square the blind ends with a chisel.

4 **Make the clips.** The clips are small wooden squares with a rabbet in one end. To make the clips, first cut a ³/₈″-wide, ³/₁₆″-deep rabbet across the *end* of the ⁵/₈″-thick stock. Cut a 1¹/₂″-wide strip off the rabbeted end of the stock, then rip this strip up into 1¹/₂″ x 1¹/₂″ squares. Drill and countersink a screw hole through the middle of each clip. Repeat until you have

made ten clips, each with a rabbet in one end as shown in the *Clip Layout*.

Note: It's important that you cut the rabbet in the *end* of each clip. (The rabbet must run across the grain.) If you cut the rabbet in the edge, the clip will be weak. A rabbeted edge will eventually break off.

5 **Drill the holes in the battens.** Each batten is attached to the underside of the shelf with three screws. Drill ³/₁₆″-diameter pilot holes with ³/₈″-diameter, ³/₈″-deep counterbores through the *edges*

of the battens. The positions of these holes are not critical, but they should be evenly spaced along the length of each batten.

6 **Cut the shapes of the aprons, battens, and shelf.** Lay out the shapes of the aprons on the stock as shown in the *Apron End Layout,* and the shapes of the battens as shown in the *Batten End Layout*. Also, mark the notches in the corner of the

shelf, as shown in the *Shelf Layout*. Cut the shapes of the aprons and battens with a band saw, scroll saw, or saber saw, then sand the sawed edges. Make the notches in the shelf with a saber saw or hand saw.

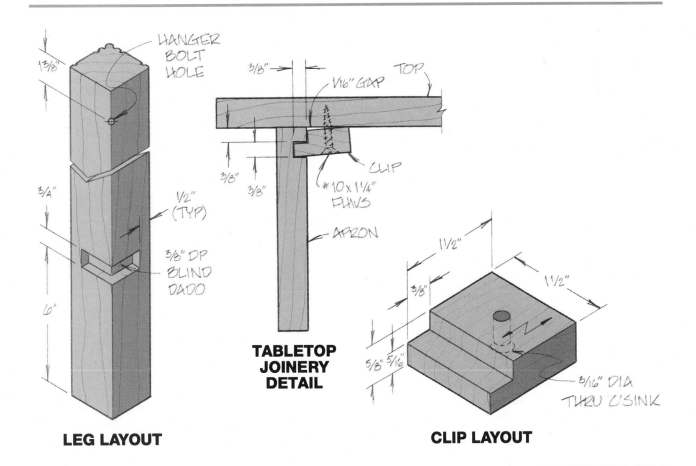

LEG LAYOUT

TABLETOP JOINERY DETAIL

CLIP LAYOUT

7

Cut the beads in the legs. The outside surfaces of the legs are cut with decorative ³/₁₆″ beads — single beads in the front, back, and side corners; and overlapping double beads in the outside corners, as shown in the *Leg Section*. Make these beads with a molder, shaper, or table-mounted router. (See Figures 8 and 9.)

8/Cut single ³/₁₆″ beads in two opposing corners in each leg — the side corner and the front or back corner. Use a three-bead cutter or knife set, but only expose one bead.

9/Cut two beads in the outside corner of each leg. Overlap these cuts so they form a single ³/₄-round bead and two ¹/₂-round beads at the corner.

8

Assemble the table. Drill ⁵/₁₆″-diameter, 1¹/₂″-deep holes in the inside corners of the legs, 1³/₈″ from the top end, as shown in the *Leg Section* and *Leg Layout*. (See Figure 10.) Finish sand the legs, aprons, top, shelf, and battens. Lightly sand the remaining parts.

Glue the hanger blocks in the apron dadoes. When the glue dries, drive the screw end of the hanger bolts into the holes in the legs. Insert the bolt ends through the holes in the hanger blocks. Secure the legs with nuts and washers. As you tighten the nuts, make sure the top ends of the legs are flush with the top edges of the aprons.

Place the top upside down on the workbench, then rest the leg-and-apron assembly upside down on the top. Position the assembly so the top will overhang the aprons 1¹/₂″ on all sides. Insert the rabbeted ends of the clips in the apron grooves. The placement of these clips is not critical, but they should be evenly spaced all around the insides of the aprons. Using the holes in the clips as guides, drill pilot holes in the underside of the top. *Be careful not to drill completely through the top!* Fasten the clips to the top with #10 x 1¹/₄″ flathead wood screws.

Spread the legs slightly and insert the shelf in the leg dadoes. (If the legs won't flex far enough to install the shelf, loosen the nuts on the hanger bolts.) Using a screw drill bit, drill an angled pilot hole (with a counterbore and countersink) through the underside of the shelf and into the leg at each corner. These holes should exit the shelf inside the leg dadoes, as shown in the *Shelf Joinery Detail,* so they won't be seen when the table is right side up. Drive #10 x 1³/₄″ flathead wood screws into the holes, fastening the shelf to the legs. Do *not* glue the shelf to the legs.

Place the battens on the shelf, as shown in the *Shelf Layout.* Using the holes in the battens as guides, drill pilot holes in the underside of the shelf. *Be careful not to drill completely through the shelf!* Fasten the battens to the shelf with #10 x 1³/₄″ flathead wood screws. Do *not* glue the battens to the shelf.

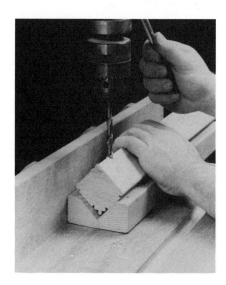

10/To hold the leg at the proper angle while you drill the hanger bolt holes, rest it in a V-block.

9 **_Finish the table._** Disassemble the table, removing the battens, shelf, legs, and top. Do any necessary finish sanding, then apply a finish to all wooden surfaces. Be sure to apply as many coats to the undersides of the top and the shelf as you do the top surfaces. This will help prevent these wide parts from cupping. Rub out the finish and buff it with paste wax, then reassemble the table.

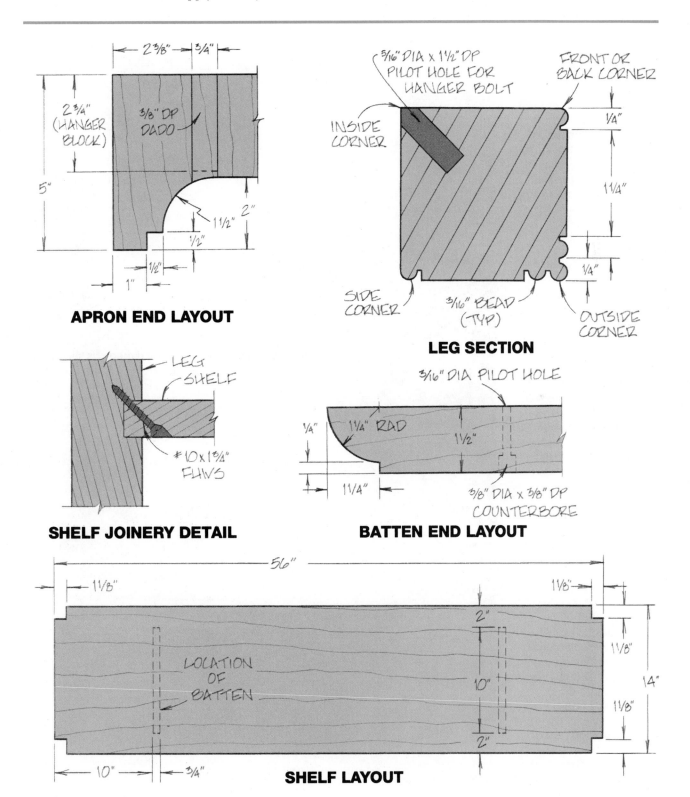

APRON END LAYOUT

LEG SECTION

SHELF JOINERY DETAIL

BATTEN END LAYOUT

SHELF LAYOUT

Progressive Windsor Chair

In the early eighteenth century, colonial chairmakers adopted the traditional English country chair and made it their own. They filled in the back with spindles and exaggerated the splayed angles of the legs. The result was the American Windsor chair, a design that has remained popular for almost three centuries.

However, it hasn't remained unchanged. American Windsor design has continued to evolve as new tools and techniques become available. Today, there is a wide range of approaches to Windsor chairmaking, from craftsmen who still build traditional, handworked chairs from green wood, to those who have updated the old designs for contemporary tastes, using modern power tools and materials.

Randall Fields belongs to the latter group. The Amesville, Ohio, woodworker counts himself as a "progressive" Windsor chairmaker, and this is one of his progressive designs. Although he carefully crafts each piece, he avails himself of every modern woodworking advantage. This chair is built from kiln-dried wood, using power tools almost exclusively. "There's a good deal of handwork in each chair," says Randall, "but it's all done with power tools."

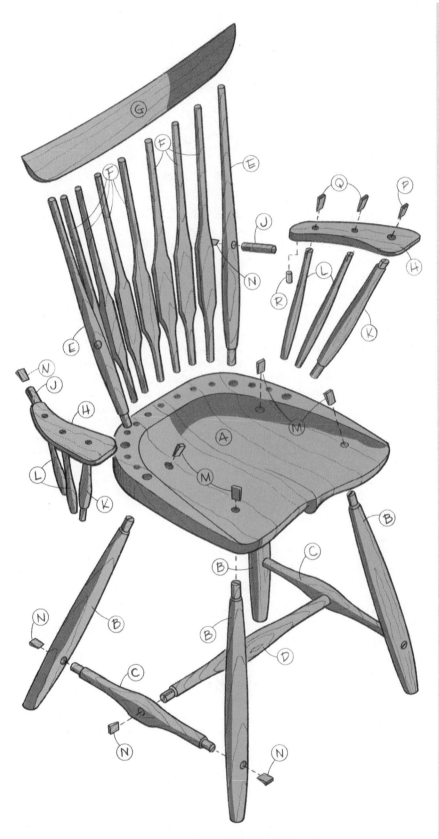

EXPLODED VIEW

Materials List

FINISHED DIMENSIONS

PARTS

A.	Seat	1⁵⁄₈″ x 17¼″ x 17¼″
B.	Legs (4)	1⁵⁄₈″ dia. x 19¼″
C.	Rungs (2)	1³⁄₈″ dia. x 16″
D.	Stretcher	1³⁄₈″ dia. x 17³⁄₈″
E.	Back posts (2)	1½″ dia. x 22¾″
F.	Back spindles (7)	½″ x 1¼″ x 22¾″*
G.	Headrest	2″ x 4⁵⁄₈″ x 24″
H.	Arms (2)	1¼″ x 3½″ x 11½″
J.	Arm dowels (2)	⁵⁄₈″ dia. x 4″
K.	Arm supports (2)	1³⁄₈″ dia. x 14″
L.	Arm spindles (4)	¾″ dia. x 12¼″*
M.	Leg wedges (4)	³⁄₃₂″ x ⁷⁄₈″ x 1½″
N.	Rung/stretcher/ arm wedges (8)	³⁄₃₂″ x ⁵⁄₈″ x 1¼″
P.	Arm support wedges (2)	³⁄₃₂″ x ½″ x 1″
Q.	Arm spindle wedges (4)	³⁄₃₂″ x ³⁄₈″ x 1″
R.	Arm pegs (2)	¼″ dia. x ⁵⁄₈″

*These are the lengths of the **longest** spindles in each set. Other spindles may be slightly shorter.*

1 **Select the stock and cut the parts to size.** To make this project, you need about 16 board feet of 8/4 (eight-quarters) stock. You can use almost any cabinet-grade wood for this chair; however, you should use a hardwood with clear, straight grain for the long, slender parts — the legs, rungs, stretcher, back posts, and spindles. American Windsor chairs were traditionally constructed from several species of domestic woods. The seats were often made from pine or poplar, the turned parts from maple, birch, or oak, and the curved parts from hickory, ash, or chestnut. On the chair shown, the seat, arms, and headrest are made from cherry, the wedges are walnut, and the remaining parts are hard maple.

Plane the rough-cut wood, removing just enough stock to see the grain. Decide which portions you will use for what parts. Cut the headrest to the dimensions specified in the Materials List. Then plane the seat stock to 1⅝" thick. Since it's difficult to find 18"-wide 8/4 stock, you'll probably have to glue up wood to make the wide board for the seat. Randall has found that he can create a pleasing grain pattern in the seat if he glues up two parts from the same 9"-wide board. He cuts the board in half, then folds one edge against itself, as shown in Figure 1. "This seam must be tight," Randall warns. "The whole chair depends on it."

Cut turning blanks for the legs, rungs, stretcher, back posts, arm supports, and arm spindles. Each blank should be 1"–2" longer than specified in the Materials

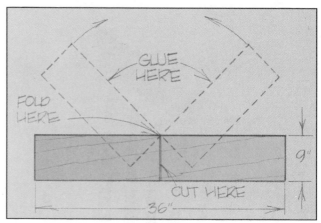

1/Select a board at least 9" wide and 36" long to make the seat. Cut the board in half and fold one edge against itself. Glue the halves together. When you cut the shape of the seat, make sure the grain runs back to front and the seam is in the middle of the seat.

List — this will give you some extra stock at either end.

The back spindles aren't turned, although they look to be. They are cut and shaped from rectangular blanks. Rip the wood for the back spindles to ⅝" thick and 1⅜" wide, then plane it to 9/16" thick. Cut the blanks 1"–2" longer than specified.

Set aside the wood for the wedges, but don't cut the wedges until you need them.

2 **Bore the mortises in the seat, headrest, and arms.** Windsor chairs, whether progressive or traditional, are built from the seat down, then the seat up. The seat, not the legs, is the foundation. So you must make the seat first.

Decide which surface of the seat stock will be the bottom, then lay out the round leg mortises and the seat shape on it, as shown in the *Seat Layout* and *Leg Mortise Layout*. Drill the leg mortises before shaping the seat. These mortises are round holes, ⅞" in diameter. They're angled so the legs splay out from the seat, as shown in the *Front View* and *Side View*.

Bore the round mortises through the seat from the bottom, using a hand-held drill and a ⅞" spade bit. To judge the angle, make a simple wire guide, as shown in the *Mortising Guide* drawing. Mark the front, back, right, and left sides of this gauge. To use it, bend the wire to the proper angle, place the guide near the mark for the mortise you want to drill, and line up the drill shaft with the wire. Bore the mortise, keeping the drill and the wire parallel. (See Figures 2 and 3.)

Note: This is not a precision operation — traditionally, craftsmen eyeball the angles of round mortises in Windsor furniture. It won't ruin the chair if the angles

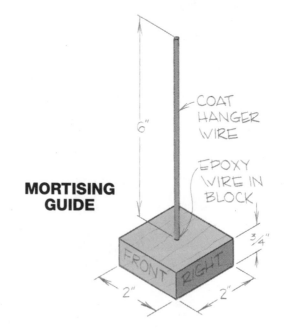

MORTISING GUIDE

are a few degrees off. Also, it doesn't matter if there's some tear-out on the top surface where the bit exits the seat. Later, you'll scoop the seat and remove the torn stock.

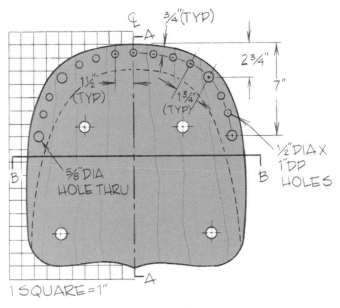

SEAT LAYOUT

1 SQUARE = 1"

BOTTOM VIEW
LEG MORTISE LAYOUT

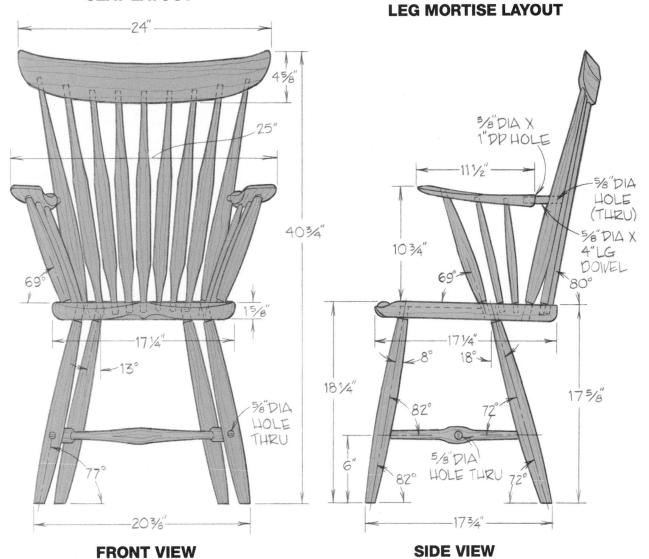

FRONT VIEW

SIDE VIEW

*2/To set the mortising guide at a compound angle, use two sliding T-bevels. Set one T-bevel to the front-to-back angle of a leg, as shown in the **Side View,** and another to the side-to-side angle, as shown in the **Front View.** Bend the wire to the proper compound angle, sighting along the edges of the T-bevels.*

3/Place the drill guide on the bottom of the seat, a few inches away from the location of the mortise to be drilled, and orient it so the front edge faces front, the right faces right, and so on. Place the point of the bit where you want to drill. Sight down the shaft and line up the drill with the wire guide as best you can. Then drill the mortise.

Turn the seat over and lay out the round mortises for the back posts, back spindles, arm supports, and arm spindles. Bore these holes from the top of the seat. Again, all of these holes must be drilled at compound angles, as shown in the *Arm and Back Mortise Layout.* Use the mortising guide to help bore the mortises at the proper angles. If you're making a set of these chairs, you may want to make several mortising guides and set them to all the different compound angles you need to bore. That way, you won't be constantly resetting the same wire guide.

4/To help bore the round mortises in the arm stock at the proper angles, mark these angles on the edge. When you drill each mortise, align the bit with the angled marks.

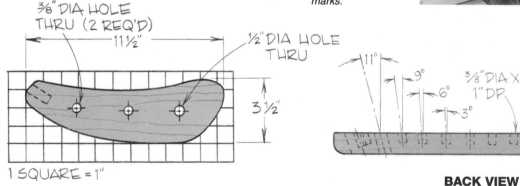

TOP VIEW

BACK VIEW

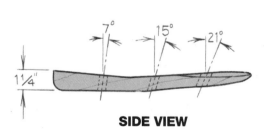

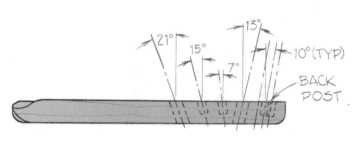

SIDE VIEW

ARM LAYOUT

SIDE VIEW

ARM AND BACK MORTISE LAYOUT

Also lay out the shapes of the arms, as shown in the *Arm Layout*. Mark the locations of the round mortises in each piece, and indicate the angles of these mortises with lines on an adjacent edge. Clamp the stock to your workbench and bore the mortises. As you do so, align the drill shaft with the angled lines on the edge. (See Figure 4.)

TRY THIS!   Randall prefers to lay out the parts and joinery with a ball-point pen — it makes a crisp, fine line with no need to be continually resharpened. It's much easier to see than a pencil, too.

3 **Carve the saddle in the seat.** Like most Windsor furniture, this chair has a "saddle" seat. The solid wood seat is carved and scooped to form a saddle shape. There are several ways to make this shape — you can use traditional hand tools, such as an inshave and scorp, a router with a ball mill, or even a hand-held circular saw. Refer to Scooping a Chair Seat for specific instructions on various techniques.

When you've chosen a tool and a technique, clamp the seat to your workbench right side up and carve the saddle. Scoop it deeper toward the back than the front, as shown in *Section A*. Near the front, leave the seat a little higher in the center than at the sides, as shown in *Section B*. This will create the "pommel" of the saddle.

Turn the seat upside down again. Using a router and a ³/₄" quarter-round bit, round over the *bottom* edges of the seat, all around the perimeter, except for the center of the front edge, just under the pommel. Using a drum

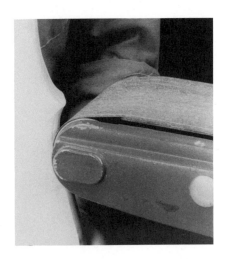

5/Sand the portion of the seat under the pommel to a point, as shown.

sander or the nose of a belt sander, shape this portion of the seat to a point. (See Figure 5.) Finish sand the bottom of the seat, but don't sand the top yet.

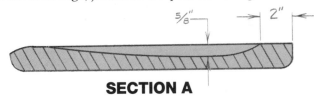

SECTION A

SECTION B

4 **Turn the legs.** Mount the leg blanks on the lathe and turn them to the shape shown in the *Front and Back Leg Layout*. Be especially careful when you turn the tenons. While other operations in making this stool leave room for slop, this doesn't. Each tenon must be precisely the specified diameter. To turn the tenons accurately, make a jig from a scrap of plywood, as shown in the *Tenon Calipers* drawing. Use this to check the diameter of the work as you turn it.

Note: To simplify the turnings, Randall makes all the tenons that go *through* another piece 2" long, and those that don't 1" long. He trims the through tenons to the proper length after he assembles the parts.

After turning all the legs, finish sand them on the lathe. Be careful *not* to sand the tenons. Also, mark the position of the rungs on the legs.

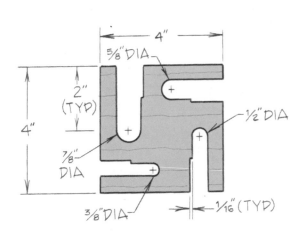

TENON CALIPERS

5 **Assemble the legs and seat.** Temporarily insert the legs in the seat. Turn them so the annual rings at the top of the legs line up with those in the seat. This will help the legs and the seat to expand and contract equally and in the same direction.

Mark the legs near the bottom end where you want to cut them off. Also, mark the *angle* of the bottom ends. Turn the assembly upside down and trim the legs with a dovetail saw or back saw.

Turn the assembly right side up and see if it sits relatively flat. (Make small adjustments later with a sander or a file.) Mark a wedge slot on the top end of each leg, where the tenon pokes through the seat. The wedges and slots must all be perpendicular to the grain direction of the seat. Also, mark the location of the legs in the seat, so you can return them to their respective mortises.

Remove the legs from the seat and cut the slots for the wedges in the tenons, using a band saw or dovetail saw. Replace the legs in the seat. Cut the wedges for the legs and lightly tap them in place. Do *not* glue the legs or wedges to the seat.

6 **Drill the rung holes.** Drill the round mortises for the rungs through the legs, using a handheld drill and a ⅝″ spade bit. Put the point of the bit on a rung mortise mark and sight along the shaft, pointing the drill at the matching mark on the other leg. Bore the mortise through the leg, then do the same at the reciprocal mark. Repeat, boring the other set of rung mortises.

7 **Turn the rungs.** Measure the distance between the front and back legs at these rung holes. If necessary, adjust the length of the rungs.

Turn the rungs as you did the legs, taking care to make the tenons precisely ⅝″ in diameter. Finish sand the rungs on the lathe, then mark the position of the stretcher holes. Cut the rungs to length. Remove the legs from the seat, install the rungs between them, then replace the legs in the seat.

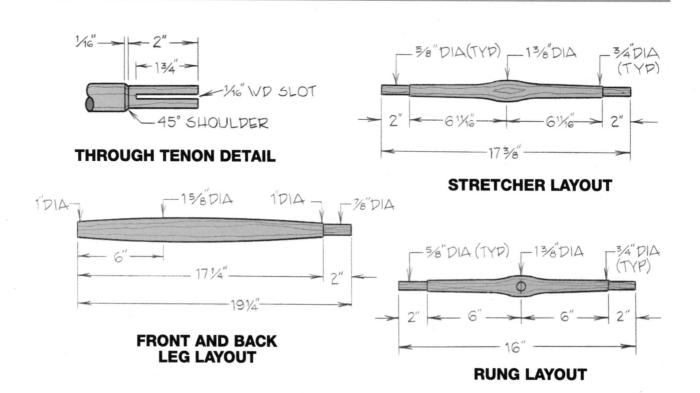

THROUGH TENON DETAIL

STRETCHER LAYOUT

FRONT AND BACK LEG LAYOUT

RUNG LAYOUT

8 **Turn and fit the stretcher.** To make the stretcher, follow roughly the same procedure for making the rungs.

Drill the round mortises for the stretcher in the rungs. Place the point of the drill on a mortise mark and sight it at the matching mark on the opposite rung. Measure between the stretcher holes. If necessary, adjust the length of the stretcher. Turn and sand the stretcher on the lathe, then install the stretcher between the rungs.

9 **Assemble the seat, legs, rungs, and stretcher.** Mark the wedge slots on the ends of the rungs and stretcher. As before, these wedges must be perpendicular to the grain direction of the surrounding wood. Mark the position of the rungs and stretcher so you can return the tenons to their respective mortises. Disassemble the legs, rungs, and stretcher, and cut the slots.

Cut the wedges for the rungs and stretcher. Using a brush, spread a little glue inside the stretcher mortises. Do *not* spread glue on the tenons — this will make it harder to clean up the glue that squeezes out of the joints. (The exceptions to this rule are the legs —

put a little glue on the leg tenons for extra insurance.) Insert the stretcher in the mortises and rotate it so the slots are properly oriented. Repeat for the rungs, then the legs.

Make sure that all the legs and rungs are in their correct positions, then wipe a little glue into each slot. Tap the wedges into the slots with a small hammer or mallet.

Let the glue dry, then cut off the protruding tenons and wedges with a coping saw or dovetail saw. Sand the ends of the tenons flush with the surfaces of the legs and seat. At the same time, finish sand the top surface of the seat, removing any tool marks.

10 **Turn the back posts, arm supports, and arm spindles.** Turn the back posts, arm supports, and arm spindles to the shapes shown in their respective layout drawings. Be careful when you turn the back posts — because these are extra long, they tend to whip and bow on the lathe. Use a lathe steadyrest to prevent them from doing so. (See Figure 6.) Once again, turn the through tenons 2″ long, and the others just 1″ long.

6/To prevent the long back posts from whipping and bowing as you turn them, support them on the lathe with a steadyrest. Many lathe manufacturers offer steadyrests as accessories. You can also make your own from a pair of casters.

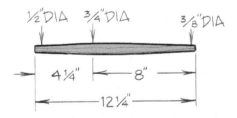

ARM SPINDLE LAYOUT

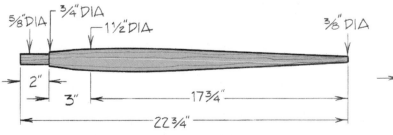

BACK POST LAYOUT

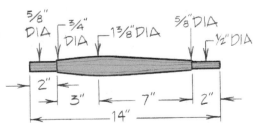

ARM SUPPORT LAYOUT

11 **Cut and shape the back spindles.**
Using a band saw and a tapering jig, cut the back spindle blanks so they taper from ⅝″ thick at the base to ½″ thick at the top. (See Figure 7.) Sand the fronts and backs of the spindles until smooth. Lay out the shape of the spindles on the front surface, as shown in the *Back Spindle Layout.* Cut the shapes with a band saw or scroll saw, then sand the sawed edges smooth.

(See Figure 8.) Be careful not to remove too much stock at this point.

Using a table-mounted router and a ¼″ quarter-round bit, round over the back edges of the spindles, cutting to within 3″ of the top ends and 1″ of the bottom ends. (See Figure 9.) Finish shaping the top and bottom portions of the spindles with a rasp, file, or similar tool. (See Figure 10.)

7/Cut the tapers in the back spindles on a band saw, using a tapering jig to guide the stock.

8/After tapering the stock, lay out the shape on the front surface. Cut the shape on the band saw.

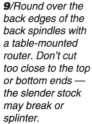

9/Round over the back edges of the back spindles with a table-mounted router. Don't cut too close to the top or bottom ends — the slender stock may break or splinter.

10/Finish shaping the tops and bottoms of the spindles by hand, rounding the ends like tenons. You can use many different tools to do this, such as a rasp, file, spokeshave, or sander, to name a few. Randall prefers to use a Surform tool, as shown.

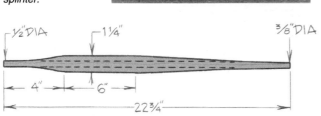

½″ DIA   1¼″   ⅜″ DIA   ½″ DIA   ⅝″   ½″   ⅜″ DIA

4″   6″

22¾″

FRONT VIEW   **BACK SPINDLE LAYOUT**   **SIDE VIEW**

12 **Shape the arms and headrest.** Enlarge the patterns of the *Headrest Layout* and trace them onto the stock. Cut the shapes of the arms and the headrest by making compound cuts on the band saw. Cut the long curves in the edges first, saving the waste. Tape the waste back to the stock, then cut the shapes in

the face of the stock. Remove the waste and the tape.

Sand the bevel on the back of the headrest with a belt sander. Also, round over the bottom edges of the arms on a table-mounted router with a ⅜″ quarter-round bit. Sand the sawed surfaces, except the top faces of the arms.

13 Fit and assemble the back parts.

Finish sand the back spindles. Then insert the back spindles and back posts in their respective mortises in the seat.

Clamp the headrest to the back posts, with the posts and spindles laying across the top face. Position the posts and spindles so they're evenly spaced. Trace the angle of the posts and spindles onto the face of the headrest, and the location of the mortises onto the bottom edge. Also mark where you will cut the spindles and posts that need to be shortened.

Remove the headrest from the assembly, clamp it to your workbench, and bore the mortises in the bottom edge. To make each mortise at the proper angle, line up the drill with the angled mark on the front face. Remove each post and spindle, and cut it to length. Saw a slot in the bottom tenon of each back post.

Replace the posts, spindles, and headrest to check the fit of the parts. When you're satisfied that they fit properly, remove the headrest and the spindles. Leave the posts in place.

14 Fit and assemble the arm parts.

Insert the arm supports and arm spindles in their respective mortises in the seat. Fit the arms over the top ends of the supports and spindles. Adjust the height and angle of the arms so they're symmetrical.

Mark the position of the arm dowel mortises on the back posts. Eyeballing the proper drill angle, bore through the back posts and into the ends of the arms. Insert the dowels in the mortises.

Mark the wedge slots on the protruding ends of the arm dowels, arm supports, and arm spindles. Disassemble the parts from the chair, cut the slots, then glue the parts in place — posts, back spindles, headrest, arms, arm dowels, arm supports, and arm spindles. Make sure that the front surfaces of the spindles are properly oriented. As you look down on them from the top of the chair, they should form a semicircle to cradle your back. Cut the wedges and tap them into the slots. Also, drill $1/4''$-diameter peg holes in the underside of the arms. Install pegs to hold the dowels in the arms.

15 Finish the chair.

When the glue dries, trim the protruding ends of the back posts, arm supports, and arm spindles flush with the bottom surface of the seat or the top surface of the arms. Finish sand all the surfaces that need it.

Apply a finish to the completed chair. Randall prefers to make his own wipe-on finish, mixing equal parts of linseed oil, tung oil, and polyurethane. Finish the entire chair, including the surfaces that won't be seen as well as those that will. Be careful to apply as many coats to the bottom of the chair seat as you do the top — this will prevent the chair from warping. After the finish dries, rub it out and buff it with wax.

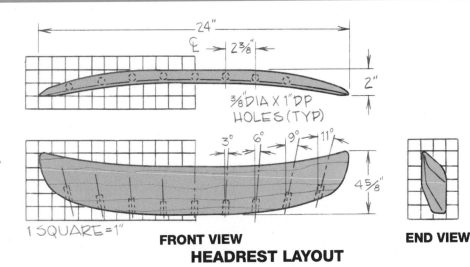

FRONT VIEW
HEADREST LAYOUT   END VIEW

Butcher Block Table

A thick, wooden butcher block tabletop offers a distinct advantage over an ordinary tabletop. You can prepare food directly on the surface, using it as a giant cutting board, without ruining the knives or the table. When the tabletop becomes scratched and stained, simply remove a thin layer of wood with a scraper or belt sander and apply a nontoxic oil finish. The table will look like new! If the top is sufficiently thick, you can refurbish the table many, many times in this manner before it becomes noticeably thinner.

This particular table offers additional advantages. First, you can build it to any height you want simply by changing the length of the legs. As shown, it's 36″ high — high enough to be used as a kitchen island. If you want to use it as a dining table, lower it to 28″–30″.

Second, you can adjust the position of the optional shelf by raising or lowering the position of the stretchers. If you want to add more shelves, install extra stretchers.

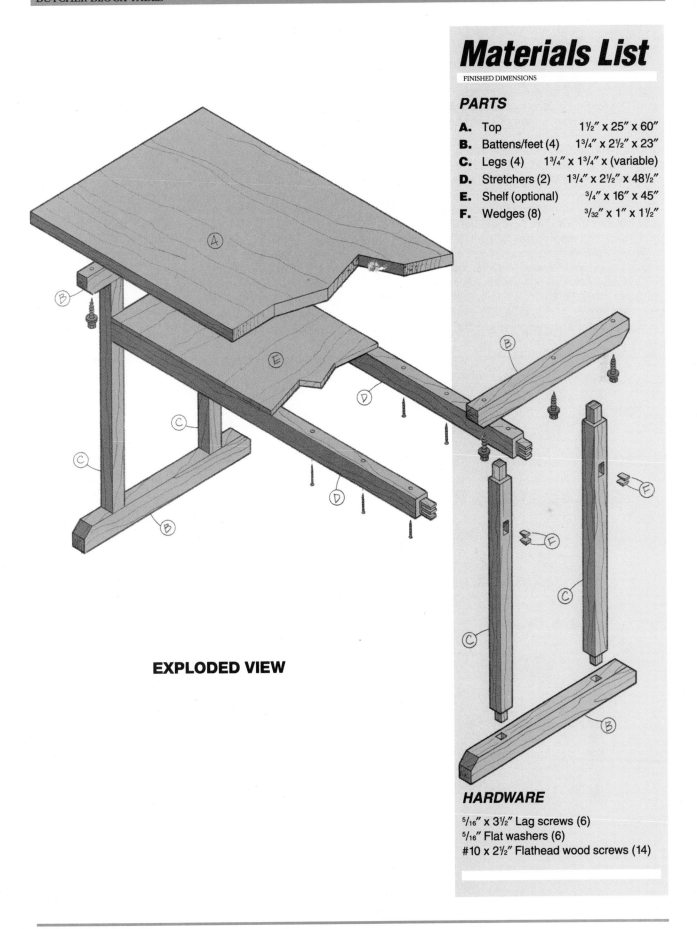

EXPLODED VIEW

Materials List

FINISHED DIMENSIONS

PARTS

A. Top $1\frac{1}{2}'' \times 25'' \times 60''$
B. Battens/feet (4) $1\frac{3}{4}'' \times 2\frac{1}{2}'' \times 23''$
C. Legs (4) $1\frac{3}{4}'' \times 1\frac{3}{4}'' \times$ (variable)
D. Stretchers (2) $1\frac{3}{4}'' \times 2\frac{1}{2}'' \times 48\frac{1}{2}''$
E. Shelf (optional) $\frac{3}{4}'' \times 16'' \times 45''$
F. Wedges (8) $\frac{3}{32}'' \times 1'' \times 1\frac{1}{2}''$

HARDWARE

$\frac{5}{16}'' \times 3\frac{1}{2}''$ Lag screws (6)
$\frac{5}{16}''$ Flat washers (6)
#10 x $2\frac{1}{2}''$ Flathead wood screws (14)

1 **Select the stock and cut the parts to size.** To make this project, you need about 7 board feet of 4/4 (four-quarters) stock, and 34 board feet of 8/4 (eight-quarters) stock. You can make this table out of almost any cabinet-grade hardwood, but most butcher block tables (including the one shown) are made from maple or birch. Avoid open-grain woods such as oak or walnut. The pores of these woods quickly absorb oils and juices from fruits, vegetables, and meats.

To save time, you may want to purchase a ready-made butcher block slab. Several lumber companies make laminated maple slabs, already planed and sanded, for use as countertops. Some even offer them already sealed and finished. You can order these through most home supply centers that sell kitchen and bathroom cabinets. The tabletop in the Materials List is a standard size — $1\frac{1}{2}$″ x 25″ x 60″ — for these ready-made countertops. If you purchase one of these slabs,

you'll only need 14 board feet of 8/4 stock to make the legs, batten, feet, and stretchers.

After selecting the wood, plane the 8/4 stock to $1\frac{3}{4}$″ thick. Cut the legs, battens, feet, and stretchers to size. Also cut one or two practice pieces $1\frac{3}{4}$″ x $1\frac{3}{4}$″ x 12″ long to test the machine setups for making the tenons. If you plan to use the table for dining, cut the legs 26″ long — this will make the completed table 29″ high. If you want to use it as a work island or counter, make the legs 33″ long — the table will be 36″ high.

If you haven't purchased the top ready-made, plane the remaining $1\frac{3}{4}$″-thick stock to $1\frac{1}{2}$″. Glue up the stock to make the tabletop. Sand it smooth, then cut it to size. If you've opted to make a shelf, plane the 4/4 stock to $\frac{3}{4}$″ thick. Glue up the stock edge to edge to make a board wide enough for the shelf. Make sure the grain runs parallel to the *short* dimension rather than the long one — side to side rather than end to end. Don't cut the shelf to size yet.

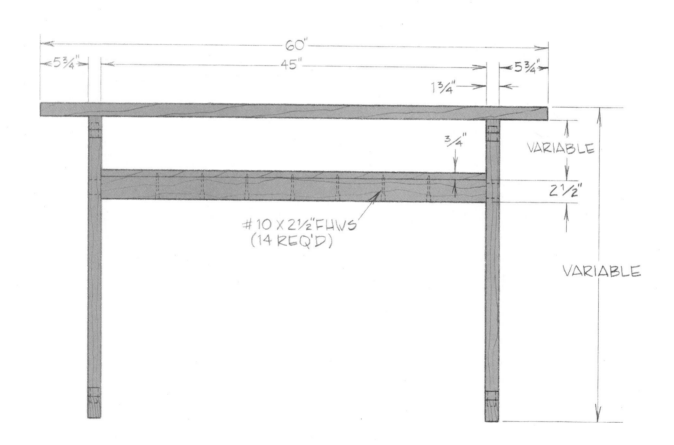

SIDE VIEW

TRY THIS! When gluing up the stock for the shelf, join the boards so that the annual rings all cup *up*. That way, if the shelf warps, it will tend to rise in the middle. You can easily control this tendency and keep the shelf flat with a few well-placed screws.

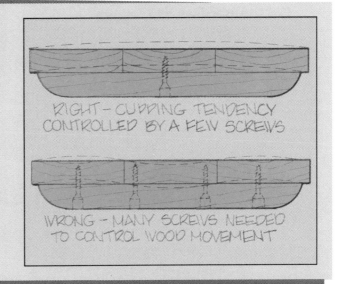

RIGHT – CUPPING TENDENCY CONTROLLED BY A FEW SCREWS

WRONG – MANY SCREWS NEEDED TO CONTROL WOOD MOVEMENT

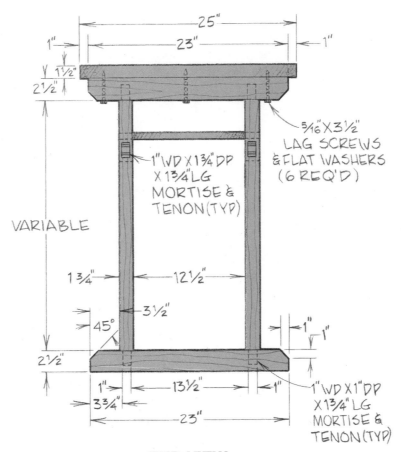

END VIEW

2 **Cut the mortises and tenons.** The table frame components — legs, feet, battens, and stretchers — are all joined by mortises and tenons. Make the mortises first, then fit the tenons to them.

Lay out the mortises on the legs, feet, and battens, as shown in the *Base Assembly Detail*. Lay out the through mortises in the legs on *both* faces of the stock. Rough out each mortise by drilling a series of overlapping 1″-diameter holes, then cleaning up the sides and squaring the corners with a chisel. (See Figures 1 and 2.) When cleaning up the through mortise, trim the waste halfway from one direction, turn the stock over, and remove the remainder from the other direction. This will prevent tear-out and keep both openings of the mortise square.

Make the matching tenons with a dado cutter or table-mounted router. Cut a 1¾″-wide, ⅜″-deep rabbet in one end of a practice piece. Turn the wood 90°, cut another rabbet, and repeat until you have cut all four sides. (See Figure 3.) The four rabbets will form a tenon on the end of the board. Test the fit of this tenon in the mortises. If it's too tight, raise the bit or cutter slightly. If the fit is too loose, lower it.

After cutting the tenons in the ends of the stretchers, cut two 1/16″-wide, 1½″-long slots for wedges in each tenon. These slots must be horizontal, so the wedges will be perpendicular to the grain direction of the legs.

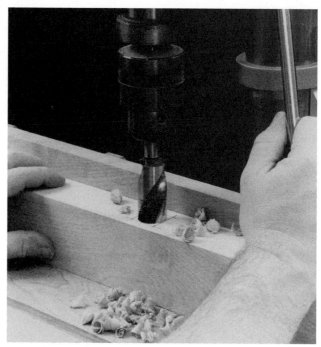

1/Rough out each mortise on a drill press, removing most of the waste by drilling a line of overlapping holes.

Use a Forstner bit if you have one; these special bits cut cleanly and leave flat-bottomed holes.

2/Clean up the sides and square the corners of each rough mortise with a chisel. When you make the final trimming cuts, clamp a thick, square block to the leg, flush

with the edge of the mortise. Rest the back of the chisel against this block as you cut — this will ensure that the sides of the mortise are perpendicular to the surface.

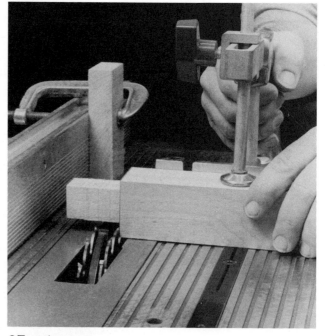

3/To make a tenon, cut four identical rabbets in the end of a board, one in each surface. Use a stop block to help gauge the length of the tenon.

3

Drill pilot holes in the battens and stretchers. The top is attached to the battens by lag screws, and the shelf to the stretchers by wood screws. Drill three ³/₈″-diameter pilot holes through the edge of each batten, and seven ³/₁₆″-diameter pilot holes through the edge of each stretcher. Counterbore the holes in the stretchers, as shown in the *Shelf Assem-* *bly Detail*. The locations of these holes don't have to be precise, but they should be evenly spaced along the length of the board.

Note that the diameters of both sets of pilot holes are slightly larger than the shanks of the fasteners. This will let the shelf and the tabletop expand and contract with changes in temperature and humidity.

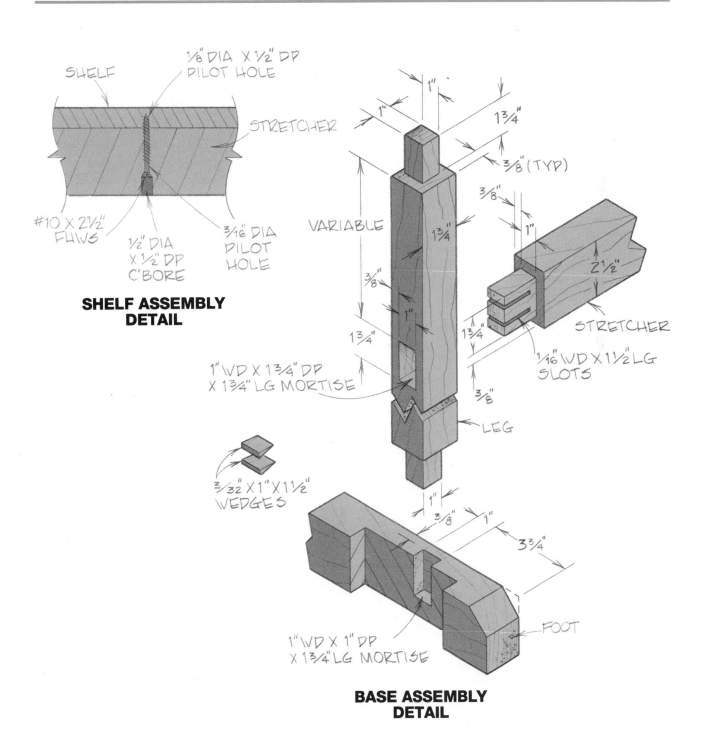

SHELF ASSEMBLY DETAIL

BASE ASSEMBLY DETAIL

4   **Chamfer the ends of the battens and feet.** Cut 45° chamfers in the ends of the battens and feet, as shown in the *End View*. Make these chamfers in the bottom corners of the battens and the top corners of the feet. Sand the sawed corners smooth.

5   **Assemble the table frame.** Finish sand the legs, battens, feet, and stretchers. Dry assemble the parts to test the fit of the mortises and tenons. When you're satisfied they fit properly, disassemble the parts and glue the legs, battens, and feet together. Let the glue dry, then join the two leg assemblies with the stretchers, gluing the tenons in the through mortises.

Before the glue dries in the through mortises, cut wedges from scrap stock. Drive the wedges into the slots in the ends of the stretcher tenons. When the glue dries, sand the ends of the tenons flush with the outside faces of the legs.

6   **Attach the shelf and top.** Carefully measure the distance between the leg assemblies and the distance between the stretchers. Either may have changed slightly from what is shown on the drawings. If this is so, adjust the dimensions of the shelf to compensate and cut it to size.

Finish sand the shelf and the top. Put the shelf in place — make sure the annual rings all cup up! Mark pilot holes in the bottom face, using the holes in the stretchers as guides. Remove the shelf and drill $\frac{1}{8}$"-diameter, $\frac{1}{2}$"-deep pilot holes in it — be careful not to drill through to the top side. Replace the shelf and secure it with wood screws.

Put the top in place, and mark the pilot holes on the bottom. Remove it and drill $\frac{5}{16}$"-diameter, 1"-deep holes at the marks. Replace the top and secure it with lag screws. Do *not* glue the top or shelf in place.

7   **Finish the table.** Do any necessary touch-up sanding, then apply a finish to the table. Be sure to apply the same number of coats to *all* surfaces — top *and* bottom. This will stabilize the shelf and the top, and help prevent them from warping.

If you intend to use the table to prepare food, apply a nontoxic finish such as mineral oil, nut oil, or salad bowl dressing. You can also use Danish oil — this becomes nontoxic after 30 days.

Variations

This design can also be adapted to make a woodworking workbench. Use the stretchers to support storage units for tools and materials — open shelves, chests of drawers, or enclosed cupboards.

Queen Anne Dining Table and Chairs

At the turn of the eighteenth century, there was a radical shift in furniture design that has affected craftsmen ever since. During the reign of Queen Anne, imported oriental furniture was all the rage among the English upper class. English cabinetmakers had been building boxy, heavy furniture of European design, but the demand for oriental furniture encouraged them to copy the flowing lines of Japanese and Chinese craftsmen. In particular, they embraced the cyma curve, also known as the S-curve or ogee. Soon an entirely new style of light, graceful furniture emerged — Queen Anne furniture.

The table and chairs shown are typical of the Queen Anne style. The cyma curve is evident everywhere — in the cabriole legs, the crest rails, even the back splats. The construction is simple and straightforward, but the skillful use of this design element makes the furniture elegant.

The dining set was built by Tom Stender of Boston, New York, who creates furniture of all styles — contemporary, traditional, and classic. "The trick to building Queen Anne furniture," Tom explains, "is to maintain a 'fair' curve when cutting or sanding a shaped part." The cyma curves must be smooth and even, with no high or low spots.

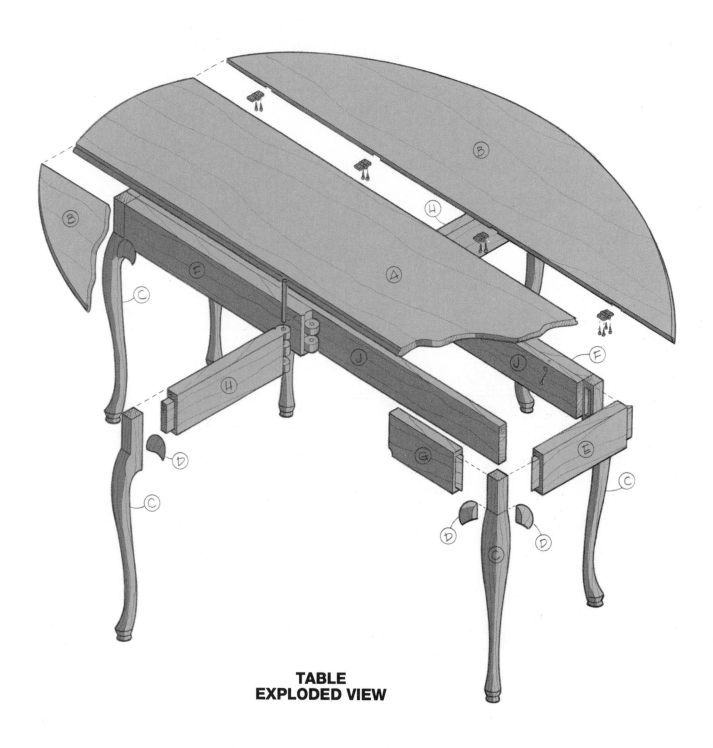

**TABLE
EXPLODED VIEW**

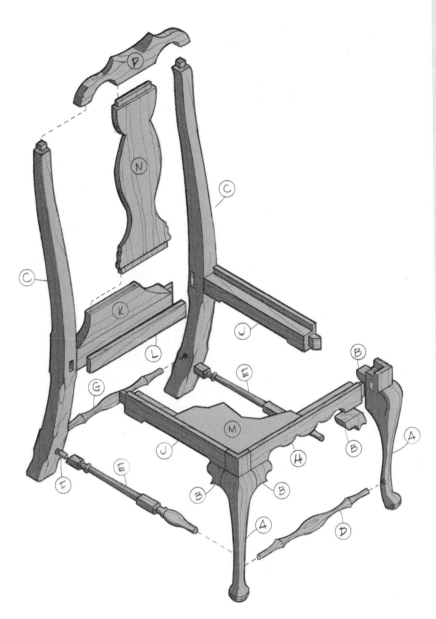

**CHAIR
EXPLODED VIEW**

Materials List

FINISHED DIMENSIONS

PARTS

Table

A.	Top	$\frac{7}{8}$" x 20" x 72"
B.	Leaves (2)	$\frac{7}{8}$" x 68" x $17\frac{1}{2}$"
C.	Legs (6)	$2\frac{7}{8}$" x $2\frac{7}{8}$" x 29"
D.	Ears (10)	$1\frac{1}{2}$" x $1\frac{1}{2}$" x $2\frac{7}{8}$"
E.	End aprons (2)	$1\frac{1}{2}$" x 5" x $14\frac{3}{4}$"
F.	Long side aprons (2)	$1\frac{1}{2}$" x 5" x $29\frac{25}{32}$"
G.	Short side aprons (2)	$1\frac{1}{2}$" x 5" x $10\frac{3}{4}$"
H.	Gates (2)	$1\frac{1}{2}$" x 5" x $18\frac{13}{32}$"
J.	Rails (2)	$\frac{3}{4}$" x 5" x 56"

Chair

A.	Front legs (2)	$2\frac{3}{4}$" x $2\frac{3}{4}$" x 17"
B.	Ears (4)	$1\frac{1}{2}$" x $1\frac{1}{2}$" x $2\frac{3}{4}$"
C.	Back posts (2)	$1\frac{3}{4}$" x $5\frac{1}{2}$" x $39\frac{1}{4}$"
D.	Front rung	$1\frac{1}{4}$" dia. x $17\frac{3}{16}$"
E.	Side rungs (2)	$1\frac{1}{2}$" dia. x $16\frac{3}{4}$"
F.	Dowels (2)	$\frac{3}{4}$" dia. x $1\frac{1}{2}$"
G.	Back rung	$1\frac{1}{4}$" dia. x $13\frac{7}{8}$"
H.	Front rail	$1\frac{3}{4}$" x $2\frac{1}{2}$" x $18\frac{3}{16}$"
J.	Side rails (2)	$1\frac{3}{4}$" x $2\frac{1}{2}$" x $16\frac{1}{4}$"
K.	Back rail	$1\frac{3}{4}$" x 4" x $14\frac{7}{8}$"
L.	Ledger	1" x 2" x $12\frac{7}{16}$"
M.	Seat	$\frac{1}{2}$" x 15" x $18\frac{3}{16}$"
N.	Back splat	$1\frac{1}{2}$" x 6" x $20\frac{3}{4}$"
P.	Crest rail	1" x $2\frac{7}{8}$" x $15\frac{7}{8}$"

HARDWARE

Table

Drop-leaf hinges and mounting screws (8)
$\frac{1}{4}$" dia. x 5" Metal pins (2)
#10 x $1\frac{1}{2}$" Flathead wood screws (12)

Chair

$\frac{1}{2}$" x 15" x $18\frac{3}{16}$" Foam pad
20" x 24" Upholstery cloth
#3 Upholstery tacks (40–50)
#10 x $1\frac{1}{2}$" Flathead wood screws (4)

Making the Table

1 ***Select the stock and cut the parts to size.*** To make the dining table, you need about 35 board feet of 4/4 (four-quarters) stock, 14 board feet of 8/4 (eight-quarters) stock, and 14 board feet of 12/4 (twelve-quarters) stock. You can make this table from almost any cabinet-grade hardwood, but classic Queen Anne furniture was traditionally made from mahogany.

In the American colonies, many eighteenth-century cabinetmakers also used domestic walnut, cherry, or maple. The dining set shown is made from walnut.

In choosing your lumber, look for straight, clear grain. Avoid figured woods. Burls and crotch figures can be very attractive, but they will also weaken a piece. The leg stock, in particular, must be free of defects —

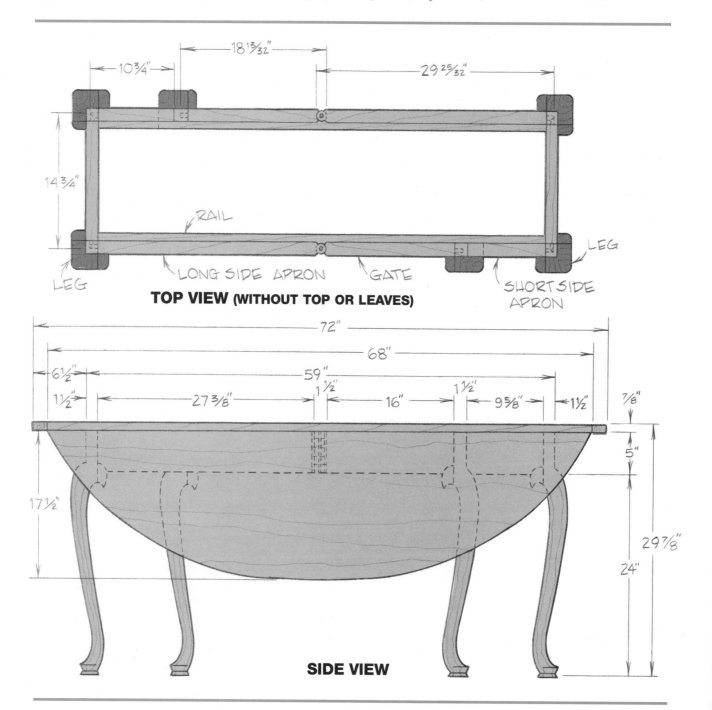

TOP VIEW (WITHOUT TOP OR LEAVES)

SIDE VIEW

cabriole legs tend to be weak at the ankles anyway. Also, consider using rift-sawn or quarter-sawn wood for the top and leaves. This lumber is more expensive than plain-sawn, but it's more stable and less prone to cupping.

Plane the 4/4 stock to ⅞″ thick, then glue up the stock needed to make the wide top and leaves. Plane the remaining ⅞″-thick stock to ¾″ and cut the rails.

Plane the 8/4 wood to 1½″ thick and cut the aprons and gates. Cut the 12/4 stock into 3″ x 3″ x 30″ leg blanks. Joint two adjacent sides of each blank to make

them 90° to one another, then plane the two remaining sides so the blanks are 2⅞″ square. Cut the blanks to 29″ long.

TRY THIS! Avoid woods with strong grain patterns, such as oak, when making Queen Anne furniture. Visually, the grain clashes with the flowing lines and the resulting piece looks "busy."

2 **Cut the mortises and tenons.** The legs are fastened to the aprons and gates with mortises and tenons. Make the mortises first, then fit the tenons to them.

To make the mortises, first enlarge the *Table Leg Pattern*. Trace the pattern on the two *inside* surfaces of each leg. Take care that these patterns line up — the post, ankle, knee, and other parts of each leg must all be precisely the same distance from the top end. You can make reference marks on your pattern to help position it on the stock.

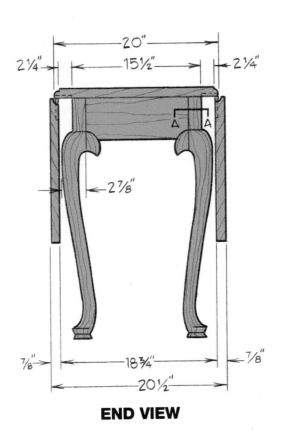

END VIEW

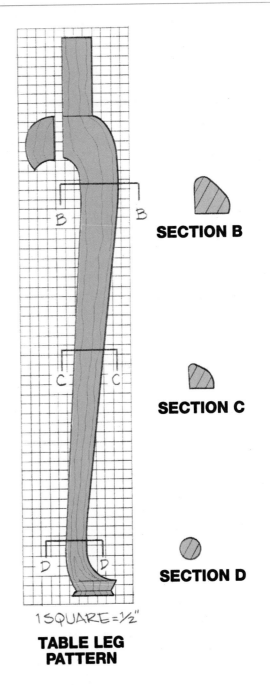

SECTION B

SECTION C

SECTION D

1 SQUARE = ½″

TABLE LEG PATTERN

Also lay out the ³⁄₄″-wide, 1¹⁄₈″-deep, 3¹⁄₂″-long mortises near the top ends of the legs, as shown in the *Leg-to-Apron Joinery Detail*. Rough out each mortise by drilling a line of overlapping ³⁄₄″-diameter holes. These mortises should meet inside each leg. (See Figure 1.) Clean up the edges and square the ends of each mortise with a chisel.

Make ³⁄₄″-thick, 1¹⁄₈″-long tenons in the ends of the aprons and gates with a dado cutter or table-mounted router. Using a dovetail saw, cut the top and bottom shoulders and miter the end of each tenon at 45°. Test fit each tenon in its respective mortise. The fit should be snug, but not too tight. Take care that it's not loose — this will weaken the table assembly.

TRY THIS! If you remove too much stock from a mortise or tenon, the joint will be loose. Replace the lost stock by gluing a thin sheet of veneer to the tenon.

*1/Cut the joinery in the legs **before** you cut the cabriole shape. It will be very difficult to make accurate joints after the legs are shaped.*

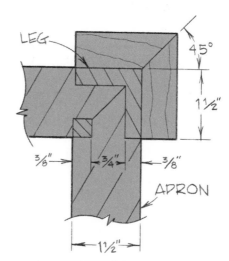

SECTION A

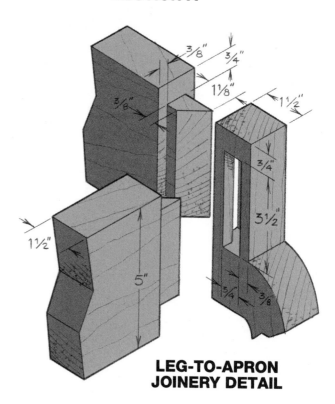

LEG-TO-APRON JOINERY DETAIL

3 Cut the shapes of the cabriole legs.

Temporarily assemble the legs, aprons, and rails. Clamp the parts together. Glue the ears to the legs, taking care not to get any glue on the aprons. Note that the gate legs only get one ear each; the others have two. When the glue sets, disassemble the parts.

Enlarge the ear pattern and trace it on the inside surfaces of the ears. Remember, the curves must be fair — they must seem to flow from the legs to the ears. Using a band saw, cut the cabriole shape in one surface of a

leg and save the waste. Adhere the waste to the leg with double-faced carpet tape, turn the stock 90°, and cut the other surface. Remove the tape and the waste. Repeat this procedure for all six legs.

Using a spokeshave or a drawknife, round over the knee, shin, and ankle of each leg, as shown in *Section B, Section C,* and *Section D*. Round the pad foot, using a dovetail saw, a rasp, and a file. For more detailed instructions on how to cut and shape a cabriole leg, refer to *Step-by-Step: Making Cabriole Legs.*

4 **Make the knuckle joints between the long aprons and the gates.** The leaves of the table are supported by a fifth and a sixth leg that swing out from underneath the table. Each of these auxiliary legs is attached to a gate, and the gate is hinged to a long side apron. This hinge is made of wood — two sets of interlocking fingers — with a metal pivot, an arrangement sometimes called a knuckle joint.

To make a knuckle joint, first lay out the shapes of the round knuckles on the top edges of the adjoining parts. Cut the shapes with a band saw, then slice the knuckles into fingers. The fingers of each apron and gate must mate. Finish shaping the knuckles with a carving chisel, then drill the holes for the pivot pins. (See Figures 2 through 6.)

4/Slice the knuckles into interlocking fingers. Cut three fingers in each gate, and two in each apron. Stop the cuts where the flat, diagonal faces meet the round knuckles. When completed, each finger should be 1" thick and 1⁹/₃₂" long.

2/Scribe 1¹/₂"-diameter circles on the top edges of the aprons and gates, near the adjoining ends. Mark the center of each circle, then draw two diagonal lines that cross in the center. Each line should be 45° from the face of the workpiece.

5/Using a carving chisel, scoop out the excess material between each finger so the fingers mate properly. Be careful not to carve into the diagonal faces.

3/Cut the shapes of the knuckles on a band saw. First cut along the diagonal lines up to each circle. (This will make a flat, diagonal face.) Then saw around the circumference of the circle, making a round knob or "knuckle" on the end of each workpiece.

*6/Fit each apron to its gate. Clamp these pieces together on a drill press and bore a ¹/₄"-diameter hole through the center of the fingers. Stop the hole when it's 4¹/₂" deep — do **not** drill through the fifth finger.*

Cut the metal pins 5″ long and install them temporarily in the joints. They should protrude about ½″ from the wood, so they will be easy to remove. Test the pivoting action — the fingers should not rub or bind. If they do, disassemble the joints and carve or file away a little stock.

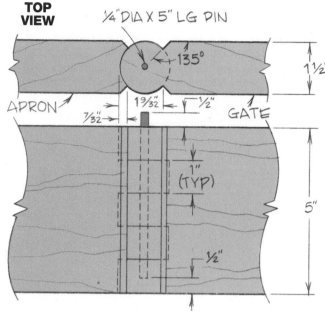

KNUCKLE JOINT LAYOUT

SIDE VIEW

5 **Cut the shapes of the short side aprons.** The lower inside corner of each short side apron must be shaped to fit around the knee of the cabriole leg. Trace this shape, using the enlarged leg pattern, then cut it with a band saw. Sand the sawed edges.

6 **Drill the screw pockets in the rails and end aprons.** The top is held to the table by flathead screws. These screws rest in screw pockets in the inside faces of the rails and end aprons. Make each screw pocket by drilling a ½″-diameter counterbore at a 15° angle, part way through the face of the wood. Then drill a ³⁄₁₆″-diameter pilot hole through the center of the counterbore. The pilot hole should exit the top edge of the workpiece, as shown in the *Screw Pocket Detail*.

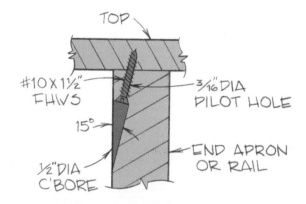

SCREW POCKET DETAIL

7 **Assemble the table frame.** Finish sand the parts you have made so far — legs, ears, aprons, gates, and rails. Glue the long side aprons and the short side aprons to the rails. Make sure the apron tenon shoulders are flush with the ends of the rails.

When the glue sets, glue the aprons, rails, legs, and ears together. Also glue the gate legs to the gates. Check that the table frame assembly is square as you tighten the clamps. Using a wet rag, wipe away any excess glue that squeezes out of the joints.

Let the glue set overnight, then assemble the knuckle joints, attaching the gate legs to the table frame. Test the pivoting action — the legs should swing in and out easily, without rubbing on the short side aprons. If they do rub, remove a little stock from the ends of the aprons with a chisel or file.

8

Make and assemble the rule joints.

The adjoining edges of the top and leaves are cut with a decorative rule joint. This joint consists of a bead or "thumbnail" in the top and a mating cove in the leaf. Cut these shapes with a shaper or router. (See Figure 7.)

Join the top and the leaves with drop-leaf hinges. Unlike most hinges, which are installed so the pin straddles the boards, drop-leaf hinges are offset slightly. One leaf of the hinge is slightly longer than the other to compensate for this offset. The exact position of each hinge is determined by the radius of the matching thumbnail and cove — the hinge pin must rest at the center of the arc.

Space the hinges evenly along the rule joints, four to a side. Calculate the proper position of each hinge pin. Rout or cut mortises for the hinges, install them, and check the folding action of the rule joints. (See Figure 8.) They shouldn't rub or bind. If they do, you may have to remove a little stock from the inside of the coves with a gouge or round scraper.

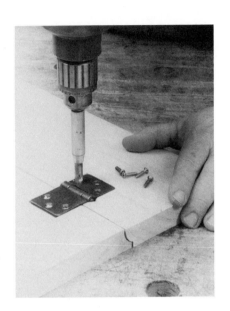

7/A rule joint consists of a thumbnail and a mating cove. You must make these shapes with two matched bits or cutters.

8/When installing a drop-leaf hinge, locate the hinge pin at the center of the rule joint arc. The hinge pin will be offset slightly toward the thumbnail side of the joint.

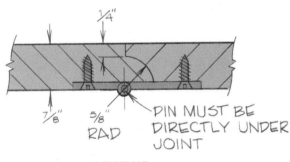

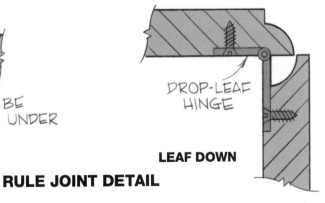

LEAF UP

LEAF DOWN

RULE JOINT DETAIL

9

Install and cut the top and leaves.

Remove the pins from the knuckle joints and replace them with $\frac{1}{4}$"-diameter dowel centers. Position the top on the table so it overhangs the end aprons by $6\frac{1}{2}$", as shown in the *Side View,* and the side aprons by $2\frac{1}{4}$", as shown in the *End View.* Press down on the top so the dowel centers leave indentations. Remove the top and drill a $\frac{3}{8}$"-diameter, $\frac{1}{2}$"-deep hole at each indentation. Replace the pins in the knuckle joints then put the top back on the table frame, fitting the holes over the pins. Secure the top to the table frame, driving screws up through the screw pockets and into the underside of the top.

Fold up the leaves and swing out the gate legs to support them. Using a string compass, lay out an oval 72″ long and 52½″ wide on the top and leaves. Drive two wire brads into the top at the foci of this oval, 11¼″ in from each end and centered between the edges, as shown in the *Top and Leaf Layout*. Make a loop of string 121½″ long and put it around the brads. Insert the point of a pencil through the knot and stretch the string taut. Draw the oval, pulling the string around the brads. (See Figure 9.)

Cut the shape of the oval with a saber saw. Sand the sawed edges.

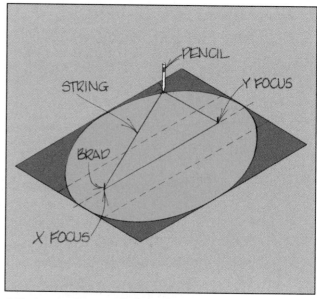

TRY THIS! To scribe an accurate oval, use a type of string that doesn't stretch easily.

9/To draw an oval, put a loop of string around two brads. Insert a pencil through the knot in the loop, stretch the string taut, and pull it around the *brads. The pencil will scribe an oval. You can change the shape and size of the oval by moving the brads or adjusting the length of the string.*

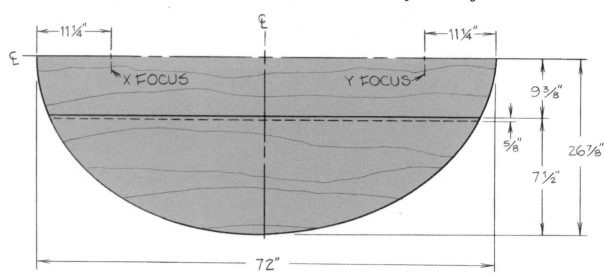

TOP AND LEAF LAYOUT

10 **Finish the table.** Disassemble the table, removing the top, leaves, and gate legs. Also remove the hinges and pins. Finish sand the top and leaves, and do any necessary touch-up sanding on the other wooden surfaces.

Apply a finish to the table, coating the surfaces that won't be seen as well as those that will. This helps keep the parts of the table from warping or cupping. Also, be sure to apply an even number of coats to all the wooden surfaces. If the finish is thinner on one side, the wood there will absorb moisture faster and expand more, causing boards to warp or cup.

When the finish dries, rub it out and apply a coat of paste wax to the table. Then reassemble the parts.

Making the Chair

11 **Select the stock and cut the parts to size.** To make each chair of this dining set, you need about 15 board feet of 8/4 stock and 2 board feet of 12/4 stock, as well as a small sheet of 1/2″ plywood and a 3/4″-diameter dowel. When selecting lumber, choose a hardwood that matches the table.

Plane the 8/4 stock to 1 3/4″ thick and cut the back posts, front rail, side rails, and back rails. Make an extra front rail and side rail to use as test pieces. Also, make turning squares for the rungs. Cut these rungs about 1″

longer than specified in the Materials List so you have a little extra stock at each end.

Plane the remaining 1 3/4″-thick stock to 1 1/2″ and cut the ears and back splat. Then plane the remaining 1 1/2″-thick wood to 1″ and cut the ledger and crest rail.

Cut the 12/4 stock into 3″ x 3″ x 18″ leg blanks. Joint two adjacent sides of each blank so they're 90° to one another, then plane the other two sides so the blank is 2 3/4″ square. Cut the blanks to 17″ long.

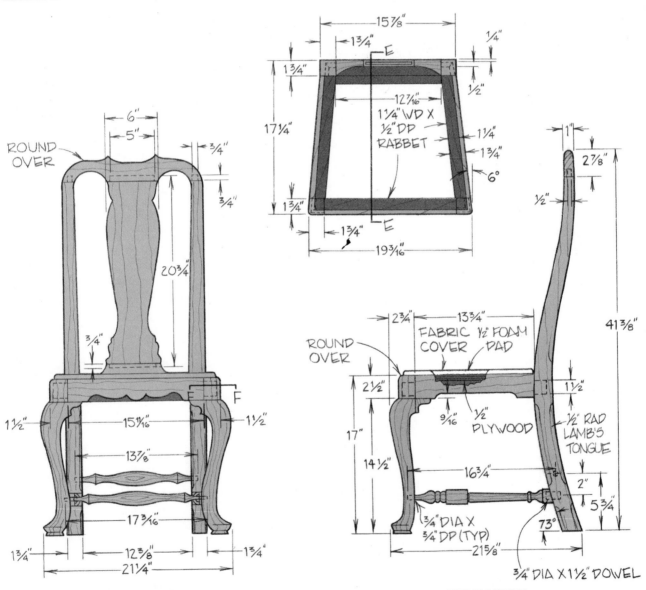

FRONT VIEW   **SIDE VIEW**

12 Make the mortises and tenons.

Make the mortises and tenons. The legs and back posts are fastened to the rails with mortises and tenons. Make the mortises first, then fit the tenons to them. Note that the mortises that hold the side rails are cut 6° off perpendicular to the surface of the wood.

To make the mortises, first enlarge the *Chair Leg Pattern.* Trace the pattern on the two *inside* surfaces of each leg. Lay out the ³/₄″-wide, 1¹/₄″-deep, 1¹/₂″-long mortises on the leg and back posts, as shown in the *Leg-to-Rail Joinery Detail* and *Side View.* Also mark the ¹/₂″-wide, ³/₄″-deep, 5″-long mortises on the back rail and crest rail and the ¹/₂″-wide, ³/₄″-deep, ⁵/₈″-long mortises on the crest rail. The longer mortises hold the back

splat in place, and the small mortises in the crest secure it to the back posts.

Rough out each mortise by drilling a line of overlapping holes. When roughing out the mortises for the side rails, drill the holes 6° off perpendicular. As with the table, each set of leg mortises and post mortises should meet inside the stock. Clean up the edges and square the ends of each mortise with a chisel.

Cut the tenons that fit in the perpendicular mortises with a dado cutter or table-mounted router. Cut the side rail tenons that fit in the angled mortises with a dovetail saw. Make a tenon in the practice rails first, then cut the good stock. (See Figures 10 and 11.) Miter the ends of the rail tenons, as shown in *Section E.*

10/Before cutting a tenon that fits an angled mortise, carefully lay out the tenon and shoulders on all four surfaces of the wood. Note that the tenon shoulders are mitered. The tenons, however, are parallel to the long dimension of the stock.

11/Cut the tenons with a dovetail saw, taking care to follow the layout lines precisely. Saw the angled shoulders first, then the top, bottom, and sides of the tenons. Miter the ends of the tenons.

13 Cut the rabbets and drill the holes.

Cut the rabbets and drill the holes. The front and side rails are rabbeted to support the seat, and the seat is secured by screws. These screws pass up through the rails and ledger and into the plywood. Drill and counterbore the screw holes first, as

shown in *Section F.* Make one hole in the center of each side rail, the front rail, and the ledger. Then make 1¹/₄″-wide, ¹/₂″-deep rabbets in the rails, using a table saw. Cut the depth of the rabbet first, then the width.

14 Cut the shapes of the rails, back posts, and back splat.

Cut the shapes of the rails, back posts, and back splat. Enlarge the *Front Rail Layout, Side Rail Layout, Back Rail Layout, Crest Rail Pattern, Back Splat Pattern,* and *Back Post Pattern.* Trace these patterns on the stock. Note that there are two patterns each for the back splat and back posts — these are compound shapes. Trace one pattern on the edge of the stock and the other on the face.

Cut a 1¹/₄″-radius cove in the top front corner of the back rail, as shown in *Section F.* Make this cove on a table saw, feeding the stock across the blade at a 60° angle. (See Figure 12.) Then cut the shapes of the parts with a band saw. On those parts with compound shapes, cut the pattern in the edge first. Tape the waste to the stock, then cut the pattern in the face.

12/To cut the cove in the back rail, feed that stock across a table saw blade at a 60° angle. Make the cove in several passes, cutting just ¹/₈″ deeper with each pass.

Round over the edges of the back posts with a router and a ¹/₂″ quarter-round bit to make the "lamb's tongues," as shown in the patterns.

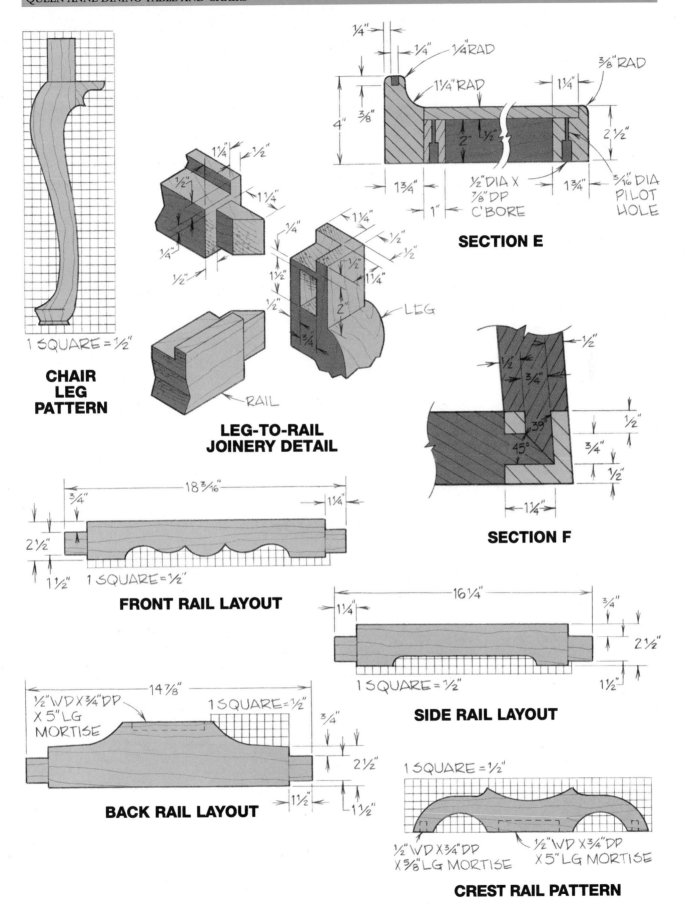

CHAIR
LEG
PATTERN

1 SQUARE = ½"

LEG-TO-RAIL
JOINERY DETAIL

RAIL

LEG

SECTION E

¼"RAD

1¼"RAD

⅜"RAD

½"DIA X
⅞"DP
C'BORE

³⁄₁₆"DIA
PILOT
HOLE

SECTION F

39°

45°

FRONT RAIL LAYOUT

18³⁄₁₆"

1 SQUARE = ½"

SIDE RAIL LAYOUT

16¼"

1 SQUARE = ½"

BACK RAIL LAYOUT

14⅞"

½"WD X ¾"DP
X 5"LG
MORTISE

1 SQUARE = ½"

CREST RAIL PATTERN

1 SQUARE = ½"

½"WD X ¾"DP
X ⅝"LG MORTISE

½"WD X ¾"DP
X 5"LG MORTISE

15

Cut the cabriole legs. Temporarily assemble the legs, back posts, splat, and rails. Clamp the parts together. Glue the ears to the legs, taking care not to get any glue on the rails. When the glue sets, disassemble the parts.

Enlarge the ear pattern and trace it on the inside surface of the ears. Using a band saw, cut the cabriole shape in one surface of a leg. Save the waste and reattach it to the leg with double-faced carpet tape. Turn the stock 90° and cut the other surface, then remove the tape and the waste. Repeat this procedure for the other leg.

Using a spokeshave or a drawknife, round over the knee, shin, and ankle of each leg. Also round the pad foot, using a dovetail saw, a rasp, and a file. For more detailed instructions on how to cut and carve a cabriole leg, refer to Step-by-Step: Making Cabriole Legs.

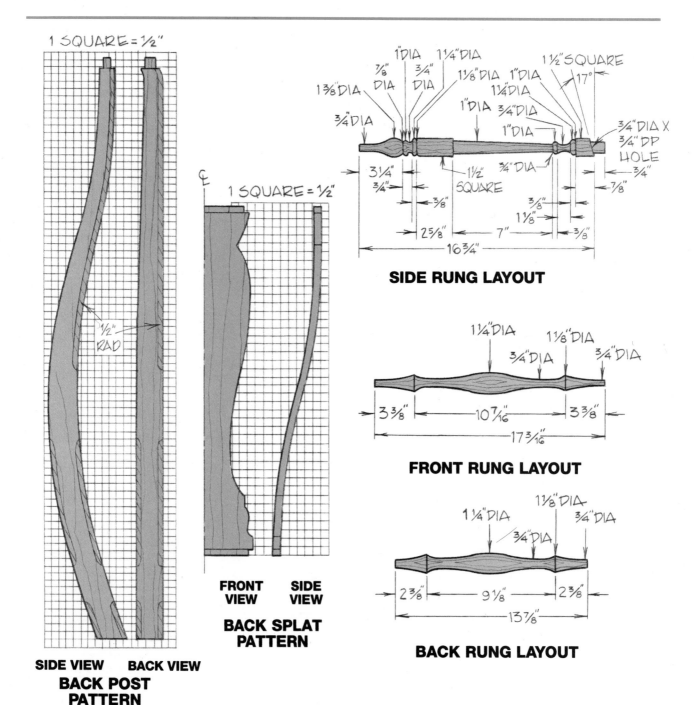

SIDE RUNG LAYOUT

FRONT RUNG LAYOUT

BACK RUNG LAYOUT

BACK POST PATTERN

SIDE VIEW　　BACK VIEW

BACK SPLAT PATTERN

FRONT VIEW　　SIDE VIEW

16

Turn the rungs. Once again, dry assemble the chair parts and clamp them together. Measure and mark the locations of the rungs on the legs, as shown in the *Front View* and *Side View*. Then measure the distance between the legs at the rung locations. Also, measure the angle of the back posts where the side rungs join them. If the dimensions or the angle have changed from what is shown in the drawings, adjust the length of the rungs or the side rung miter angle accordingly.

Turn the shapes of the rungs, as shown in the *Front Rung Layout, Side Rung Layout,* and *Back Rung*

Layout. Take care to turn the tenons on the ends of the rungs to precisely ³/₄″ in diameter. Finish sand the rungs on the lathe, then cut them to size. Miter the back ends of the side rungs and bore ³/₄″-diameter, ³/₄″-deep holes in the mitered ends.

Disassemble the chair parts and drill the round mortises for the rungs. "Eyeball" the proper angle for these mortises; don't worry if they're off a few degrees — it won't adversely affect the chair. Cut two ³/₄″-diameter, 1¹/₂″-long dowels and glue them in the back ends of the side rungs. Dry assemble the chair parts one last time to check the fit of the rungs.

17

Assemble the chair. Disassemble the chair and finish sand all the parts except the rungs. Round over the top edges of the rails where shown in the *Front View, Side View,* and *Section F.*

Reassemble the parts with glue. Carefully check the angle of the rails, legs, and back posts as you clamp the parts together — make sure the seat is symmetrical.

Wipe away any glue that squeezes out of the joints with a wet rag.

When the glue dries, remove the clamps. Miter the ends of the ledger at 84° and glue it to the inside surface of the back rail. The top edges of the ledger must be flush with the rabbets in the side rails.

18

Fit the chair seat. The seat rests on the ledges created by the ledger and the rabbeted rails. To make this ledge continuous all around the perimeter of the seat, rout out a notch in the top end of each leg, as shown in the *Leg-to-Rail Joinery Detail.*

Trim the corners of the notches with a hand chisel.

Cut a piece of cabinet-grade ¹/₂″ plywood to fit the ledge. The fit must be fairly loose, leaving about ¹/₁₆″–¹/₈″ of slop all around the seat. This will leave room for the upholstery.

19

Upholster the seat. Adhere a ¹/₂″-thick foam pad to the top surface of the plywood seat with a spray adhesive. Cut the seat upholstery to size and turn it upside down on a clean surface. Turn the foam-covered seat upside down on top of it.

Fold the back edge of the seat covering over the plywood and tack it in place. Repeat at the front edge, stretching the upholstery taut. (See Figure 13.)

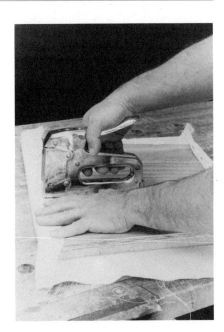

13/Attach the upholstery to the bottom of the foam-covered seat with tacks or staples. Start at the back edge, then do the front. Stretch the upholstery tight enough to round over the edges of the foam pad.

Then do the same for the side edges. Neatly fold the upholstery at the corners so the cloth won't look gathered or bunched up. (See Figure 14.) When you turn the upholstered seat over, the cloth covering should be perfectly smooth and rounded at the edges.

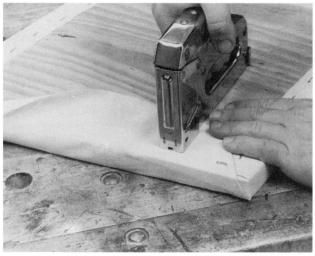

14/When you tack the sides of the upholstery in place, neatly fold the material at the corners. If you don't, the upholstery on top of the seat will look bunched up.

20 **Finish the chair.** Do any necessary shaping and touch-up sanding to the wooden parts of the chair. Apply the same finish to the chair that you did to the table, rub it out, and buff it with wax. When the finish dries, place the upholstered seat in the chair. Secure it by driving screws up through the rails and ledger and into the plywood.

Step-by-Step: Making Cabriole Legs

In the seventeenth century, imported oriental furniture was all the rage in Europe. Fashion-conscious clients requested that European craftsmen incorporate Chinese and Japanese designs in their own furniture. Among the most distinctive designs was the graceful, S-shaped cabriole leg. This proved immensely popular, and by the eighteenth century the cabriole leg was commonplace in Europe and its colonies.

The curves in a cabriole leg are made with compound cuts — a series of cuts in two or more faces of the stock. Old-time craftsmen used a fretsaw to make these cuts; most contemporary furnituremakers use a band saw.

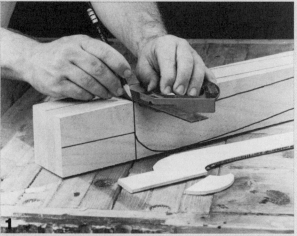

1

Trace the cabriole shape onto the two adjacent inside faces of the leg stock. Lay out and cut the joinery in the leg before you saw the curves — it will be almost impossible to make accurate joints after the leg is shaped.

Step-by-Step: Making Cabriole Legs — Continued

2

With the stock resting on the outside faces, cut the "post" — the rectangular portion at the top of the cabriole leg. Don't cut the waste free — just saw down to the "knee," where the curved shape begins.

3

If your cabriole leg design has wings or "ears," glue the blocks to the inside faces of the stock after you cut the joinery. Trace the shape on the inside faces of the ears.

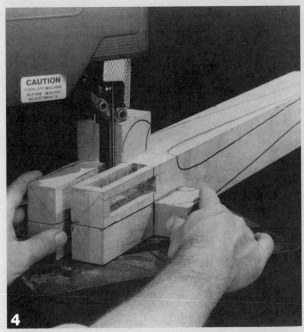

4

Rest the stock on one of its outside faces and raise the upper blade guide to clear the ear block. Cut the curve of the knee, freeing the waste from one side of the post. Save the scrap.

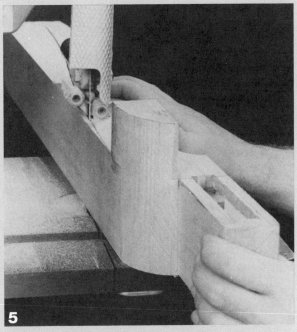

5

Lower the blade guide again and cut the remaining curves in the leg, sawing up to the knee. Once again, save the scrap.

(Continued)

Step-by-Step: Making Cabriole Legs — Continued

6

Tape the scrap back to the leg, making the stock rectangular again. Turn the leg so it rests on the other outside face, then make the same sequence of cuts. When you remove the waste and the tape, the leg will have the distinctive cabriole shape.

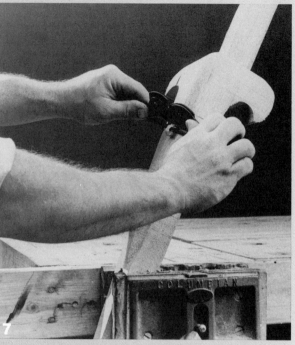

7

Finish shaping the leg by hand. Round the hard corners of the knee, taper, and ankle with a spokeshave, file, and scraper.

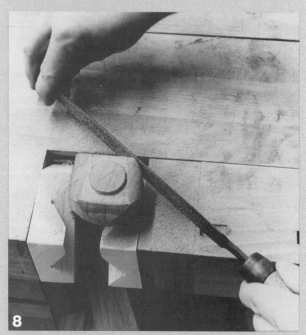

8

Knock off the corners of the foot with a saw, then round it with a rasp and file. Blend the top of the foot into the ankle.

Credits

About the Author: Nick Engler is a contributing editor to *American Woodworker* magazine, and teaches wood craftsmanship and technology at the University of Cincinnati. He has written over 20 books on woodworking.

Contributing Craftsmen and Craftswomen:

Larry Callahan (Extension Table)

Judy Ditmer (Generic Table)

Nick Engler (Shaker Bench, Cottage Rocker, Butcher Block Table)

Mary Jane Favorite (Sofa Table)

Randall Fields (Progressive Windsor Chair, Three-Legged Stool)

Lewis Gay (Dining Booth)

John Parsons (Occasional Table)

Tom Stender (Queen Anne Dining Table and Chairs)

Note: One project, the Harvest Table, was built by a woodworker whose name has been erased by time. We regret that we cannot tell you who built it; we can only admire his (or her) craftsmanship.

The designs for the projects in this book (that are attributed to a designer or builder) are the copyrighted property of the craftsmen and craftswomen who made them. Readers are encouraged to reproduce these copyrighted projects for their personal use or for gifts. However, reproduction for sale or profit is forbidden by law.

Special Thanks To:

Dave Arnold

Sam and Alpha Bundy

Bob Menker

Howard and Barbara Rothenberg

Fred and Becky Sacks

Wertz Hardware Store, West Milton, Ohio

Rodale Press, Inc., publishes AMERICAN WOODWORKER™, the magazine for the serious woodworking hobbyist. For information on how to order your subscription, write to AMERICAN WOODWORKER™. Emmaus, PA 18098.

WOODWORKING GLOSSARY

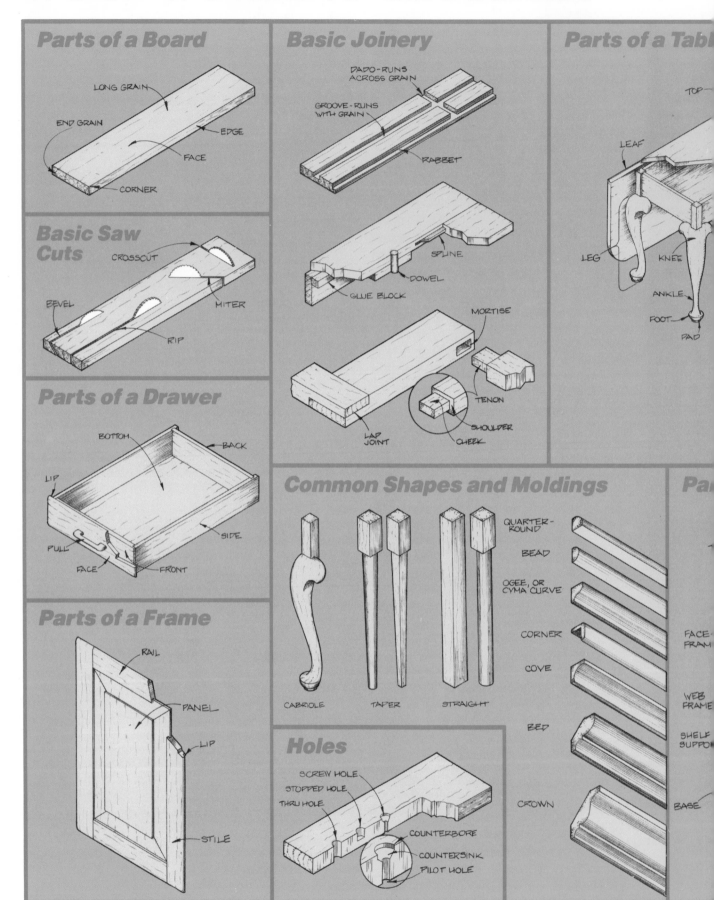

Parts of a Board

LONG GRAIN
END GRAIN
EDGE
FACE
CORNER

Basic Saw Cuts

CROSSCUT
BEVEL
MITER
RIP

Parts of a Drawer

BOTTOM
BACK
LIP
SIDE
PULL
FACE
FRONT

Parts of a Frame

RAIL
PANEL
LIP
STILE

Basic Joinery

DADO - RUNS ACROSS GRAIN
GROOVE - RUNS WITH GRAIN
RABBET
SPLINE
DOWEL
GLUE BLOCK
MORTISE
TENON
SHOULDER
CHEEK
LAP JOINT

Parts of a Tabl[e]

TOP
LEAF
LEG
KNEE
ANKLE
FOOT
PAD

Common Shapes and Moldings

QUARTER-ROUND
BEAD
OGEE, OR CYMA CURVE
CORNER
COVE
BED
CROWN
CABRIOLE
TAPER
STRAIGHT

Holes

SCREW HOLE
STOPPED HOLE
THRU HOLE
COUNTERBORE
COUNTERSINK
PILOT HOLE

Pa[r]

FACE-FRAM[E]
WEB FRAME
SHELF SUPPO[RT]
BASE